ISBN: 978-0-9983722-0-4

# ACKNOWLEDGEMENTS

I am deeply grateful to the following people: my family-Sasha, Igor, and Yura-who led the way; my wife-Julia-who inspires and supports me; the teachers, coaches, and colleagues who believed in me and demanded my best; and the friends who ground me.

# CONTENTS

# INTRODUCTION

When I was first introduced to the Common Core Standards, I remember becoming concerned about the future of my curriculum. I had taught some of the new standards, but I had no experience with many of them. The sheer quantity was daunting, because in many grade levels teachers are asked to teach over 60 standards in 180 school days, averaging to about 3 days of instruction per standard. In addition, Common Core involves basing instruction and assessment upon precise, cognitively-demanding outcomes requiring higher-level thinking skills such as critical analysis and comprehensive evaluation. Even the most skillful teacher would be challenged by this overwhelming quantity and rigor.

Therefore, like many educators, it's no wonder I felt apprehensive when first contemplating how to implement Common Core. I had many questions on my mind: How am I going to teach over 60 standards in a school year? How am I going to engage students and keep them engaged? It seemed like a challenge without a clear solution at the time, but after months of ideation, I came to a promising approach. It is indeed possible to tackle this quantity and rigor but only with the right tool-one that is based on the proven principle of visual instruction coupled with the decomposition of the standards. Research has proved the positive effects of visual instruction by demonstrating that 65% of the population learns visually[1], and graphic organizers have positive effects on reading comprehension, student achievement, thinking and learning skills, retention, and cognitive learning theory[2]. I strongly believe that leveraging this visually based concept in classrooms will allow teachers to help their students master the rigorous demands of Common Core.

## **Content**

I developed this book to intricately depict the concept of visual learning and to serve as a comprehensive set of graphic organizers and example guides for the grades 6-12 English, History/Social Studies, and Science/Technical standards. Each page provides a carefully crafted visual model that captures the variables inherent in each standard and allows teachers to precisely target the intended skill(s) of the standard. Therefore, each page consists of an explanation of a standard(s), the corresponding visual instructional tool representing that standard(s) (e.g., a graphic organizer or example guide), and detailed instructions on how to use it for its intended purpose.

For easy use, this book is organized into five sections according to grade level:

- 6th grade
- 7th grade
- 8th grade
- 9th-10th grade
- 11th-12th grade

Each section has a chapter on Common Core's language modalities and disciplines:

- Reading Informational Text
- Reading Literature Text
- Writing
- Speaking/Listening
- Language
- History/Social Studies
- Science/Technical

## **Users**

Teachers can use this book as a supplement to their existing strategies to create more efficiency and effectiveness in managing the quantity and precision that Common Core demands. Specifically, the graphic organizers and example guides can be leveraged in modeling, guided and independent practice, formative and summative assessment, portfolios, projects, and as a basis for feedback. I believe that these tools will help teachers more easily guide students down the path of mastery, achievement, and growth. Additionally, I hope that parents can also utilize this book as a guide to understand their children's learning outcomes so that they can partner with teachers and get more effectively involved in the academic success of their children.

# Section 1

6th Grade

Graphic Organizers

# CHAPTER 1

# 6th Grade
# Reading Informational Text

# CCSS.ELA-Literacy.RI.6.1

Cite textual evidence to support analysis of what the text says explicitly as well as inferences drawn from the text. *

## Explanation

This standard asks students to indicate proof of explicit and inferential meaning within an informational text. With this graphic organizer, students are able to analyze for explicit and inferential meaning in the top row and relate evidence for those individual meanings in the bottom row.

| Explicit Meaning | |
|---|---|
| **Textual Evidence** | |

| Inferential Meaning | |
|---|---|
| **Textual Evidence** | |

## CCSS.ELA-Literacy.RI.6.2

Determine a central idea of a text and how it is conveyed through particular details; provide a summary of the text distinct from personal opinions or judgments.*

## Explanation

This standard asks students to establish the essential idea and details of an informational text, then summarize. With this graphic organizer, students are able to express the central idea in the big box at the top and related details in the small boxes. Space is provided for a summary as well.

**Central Idea**

| | | |
|---|---|---|
| Detail 1 | Detail 2 | Detail 3 |
| Detail 4 | Detail 5 | Detail 6 |

**Summary:**

_____

_____

_____

_____

_____

_____

_____

## CCSS.ELA-Literacy.RI.6.3

Analyze in detail how a key individual, event, or idea is introduced, illustrated, and elaborated in a text (e.g., through examples or anecdotes).*

## Explanation

This standard asks students to examine how a topic in an informational text is initiated, visualized, and detailed. With this graphic organizer, students are able to write the name of a key individual, event, or idea in the first row and relate how it is introduced in the second row, illustrated in the third row, and elaborated in the fourth row.

| Key Individual/ Event/ Idea | | |
|---|---|---|
| **Introduction** | | |
| **Illustration** | | |
| **Elaboration** | | |

# CCSS.ELA-Literacy.RI.6.4

Determine the meaning of words and phrases as they are used in a text, including figurative, connotative, and technical meanings.*

## Explanation

This standard asks students to establish different meanings for words and phrases in an informational text. With this graphic organizer, students are able to write the words or phrases in the left column and relate various meanings in the right column.

| Words/Phrases | Meanings |
|---|---|
| | Figurative- <br><br> Connotative- <br><br> Technical- |
| | Figurative- <br><br> Connotative- <br><br> Technical- |
| | Figurative- <br><br> Connotative- <br><br> Technical- |

# CCSS.ELA-Literacy.RI.6.5

Analyze how a particular sentence, paragraph, chapter, or section fits into the overall structure of a text and contributes to the development of the ideas.*

## Explanation

This standard asks students to examine how a particular piece of an informational text functions as a part of a text structure and how it adds to the development of the ideas. With this graphic organizer, students are able to write the particular parts of an informational text in the left column, relate structural fit in the middle column, and explain contribution to the development of ideas in the right column.

| Sentence/ Paragraph/ Chapter/ Section | Fit Within Text Structure (Choose One: Chronological/Sequence, Cause/Effect, Problem/Solution, Compare/Contrast, Description, Directions) | Contribution to Idea Development |
|---|---|---|
|  |  |  |
|  |  |  |

# CCSS.ELA-Literacy.RI.6.6

Determine an author's point of view or purpose in a text and explain how it is conveyed in the text.*

## Explanation

This standard asks students to establish an author's point of view or purpose in an informational text and detail how it is communicated. With this graphic organizer, students are able to write the author's point of view or purpose in the left column and relate evidence of how it is conveyed in the right column.

| Author's Point of View/Purpose | How Point of View/Purpose is Conveyed |
|---|---|
| | Evidence- <br><br> Evidence- <br><br> Evidence- <br><br> Evidence- |

## CCSS.ELA-Literacy.RI.6.7

Integrate information presented in different media or formats (e.g., visually, quantitatively) as well as in words to develop a coherent understanding of a topic or issue.*

## Explanation

This standard asks students to combine various informational material and express what they have comprehended. With this graphic organizer, students are able to identify information presented in different media, formats, or words in the top three boxes and use that information to communicate comprehension in the box at the bottom.

| **Visual** | **Quantitative** | **Verbal** |
|---|---|---|
| | a. | a. |
| | b. | b. |
| | c. | c. |
| | d. | d. |

**Understanding of Topic/Issue**

# CCSS.ELA-Literacy.RI.6.8

Trace and evaluate the argument and specific claims in a text, distinguishing claims that are supported by reasons and evidence from claims that are not.*

## Explanation

This standard asks students to dissect an informational text's argument or claim in terms of reasons and evidence, then assess which claims are supported and which claims are not. With this graphic organizer, if the argument or claim can be supported, then the claim is written in the top left box and the reasons/evidence are written in the left column. If the argument or claim can't be supported, then the claim is written in the top right box and the reasons/evidence are written in the right column.

| Argument/Claim | Argument/Claim |
|---|---|
| | |

| Supporting Reasons/Evidence | Unsupported Reasons/Evidence |
|---|---|
| Reasons- | Reasons- |
| Evidence- | Evidence- |

*The Visual Edge©*

## CCSS.ELA-Literacy.RI.6.9

Compare and contrast one author's presentation of events with that of another (e.g., a memoir written by and a biography on the same person).*

## Explanation

This standard asks students to note the similarities and differences of two informational authors' text on the same topic. With this graphic organizer, students are able to write the authors' names at the top and identify a characteristic of both texts in the boxes on the left. Then, based on that characteristic, differences are written in the non-intersecting parts of the circles, and similarities are written inside the intersection of the two circles.

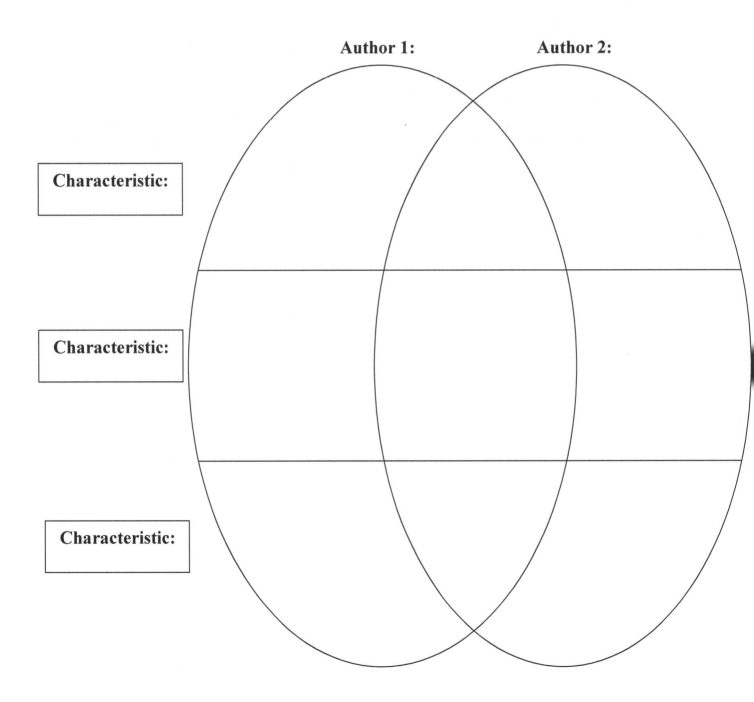

## CCSS.ELA-Literacy.RI.6.10

By the end of the year, read and comprehend literary nonfiction in the grades 6–8 text complexity band proficiently, with scaffolding as needed at the high end of the range.*

## Explanation

This standard asks students to read non-fiction texts that are grade-level appropriate. No table or graphic organizer is applicable.

# CHAPTER 2

# 6th Grade
# Reading Literature Text

# CCSS.ELA-Literacy.RL.6.1

Cite textual evidence to support analysis of what the text says explicitly as well as inferences drawn from the text.*

# Explanation

This standard asks students to indicate proof of explicit and inferential meaning within a literature text. With this graphic organizer, students are able to analyze for explicit and inferential meaning in the top row and relate evidence for those individual meanings in the bottom row.

| **Explicit Meaning** | |
| --- | --- |
| **Textual Evidence** | |

| **Inferential Meaning** | |
| --- | --- |
| **Textual Evidence** | |

# CCSS.ELA-Literacy.RL.6.2

Determine a theme or central idea of a text and how it is conveyed through particular details; provide a summary of the text distinct from personal opinions or judgments.*

## Explanation

This standard asks students to establish the essential idea and details of a literature text, then summarize. With this graphic organizer, students are able to express the theme or central idea in the big box at the top and related details in the small boxes. Space is provided for a summary as well.

## Theme/Central Idea

|  |
|--|
|  |

| Detail 1 | Detail 2 | Detail 3 |
|----------|----------|----------|
|  |  |  |

| Detail 4 | Detail 5 | Detail 6 |
|----------|----------|----------|
|  |  |  |

## Summary:

_____

_____

_____

_____

_____

_____

_____

# CCSS.ELA-Literacy.RL.6.3

Describe how a particular story's or drama's plot unfolds in a series of episodes as well as how the characters respond or change as the plot moves toward a resolution.*

## Explanation

This standard asks students to explain a story's or drama's events and character reactions that lead to a conclusion. With this graphic organizer, students are able to write the name of the story/drama at the top and document these story elements in a timeline format below.

## Name of Story/Drama:

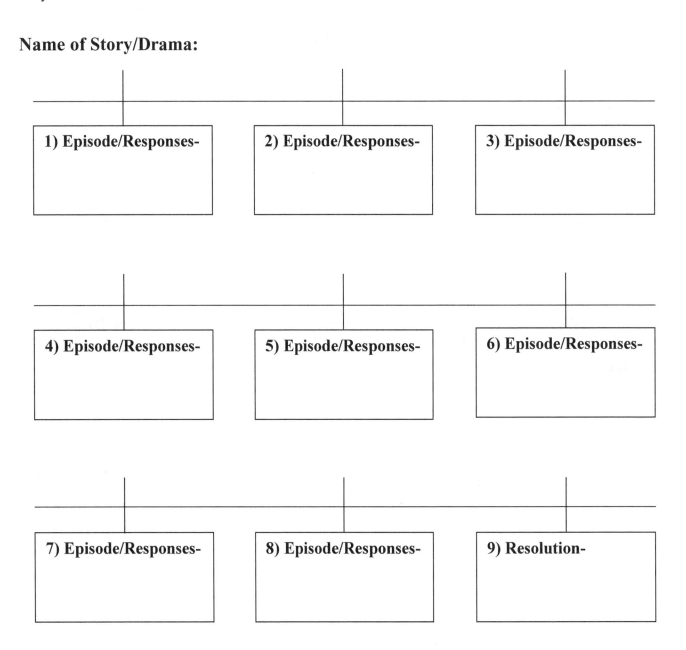

1) Episode/Responses-

2) Episode/Responses-

3) Episode/Responses-

4) Episode/Responses-

5) Episode/Responses-

6) Episode/Responses-

7) Episode/Responses-

8) Episode/Responses-

9) Resolution-

# CCSS.ELA-Literacy.RL.6.4

Determine the meaning of words and phrases as they are used in a text, including figurative and connotative meanings; analyze the impact of a specific word choice on meaning and tone.*

# Explanation

This standard asks students to establish different meanings for words and phrases in a literature text and determine their relation to meaning and tone. With this graphic organizer, students are able to use the left table to write a word or phrase in the first column and describe its various definitions in the second column. Students are able to use the right table to write a specific word choice in the first column and analyze its impact on meaning and tone in the second column.

| Word/ Phrase | Definition |
|---|---|
| | Figurative- |
| | |
| | Connotative- |

| Specific Word Choice | Impact Analysis |
|---|---|
| | Meaning- |
| | |
| | Tone- |

# CCSS.ELA-Literacy.RL.6.5

Analyze how a particular sentence, chapter, scene, or stanza fits into the overall structure of a text and contributes to the development of the theme, setting, or plot.*

# Explanation

This standard asks students to examine how a particular part of a literature text functions as a part of the text's structure and determine its development contribution on specific story elements. With this graphic organizer, students are able to write the particular part of the literature text in the left column, relate its structural fit in the middle column, and explain its development contribution to theme, setting, or plot in the right column.

| Sentence/ Chapter/ Scene/ Stanza | Fit Within Text Structure (Choose One: Setup, Conflict, or Resolution) | Development Contribution (Choose One: Theme, Setting, or Plot) |
|---|---|---|
|  |  |  |
|  |  |  |

# CCSS.ELA-Literacy.RL.6.6

Explain how an author develops the point of view of the narrator or speaker in a text.*

## Explanation

This standard asks students to describe the way an author builds speaker or narrator point of view in a literature text. With this graphic organizer, students are able to write the speaker's or narrator's point of view in the left column and relate how it develops through specific story episodes in the right column.

| Narrator's/ Speaker's Point of View | Development |
|---|---|
| | **Episode-** |
| | **Episode-** |
| | **Episode-** |
| | **Episode-** |

# CCSS.ELA-Literacy.RL.6.7

Compare and contrast the experience of reading a story, drama, or poem to listening to or viewing an audio, video, or live version of the text, including contrasting what they "see" and "hear" when reading the text to what they perceive when they listen or watch.*

## Explanation

This standard asks students to note the similarities and differences of reading a literature text with viewing or hearing it. With this graphic organizer, students are able to write the text title at the top and a characteristic of both text modes in the boxes on the left. Then, based on that characteristic, differences are identified in the non-intersecting parts of the circles, and similarities are identified in the intersection of the two circles.

**Text:**

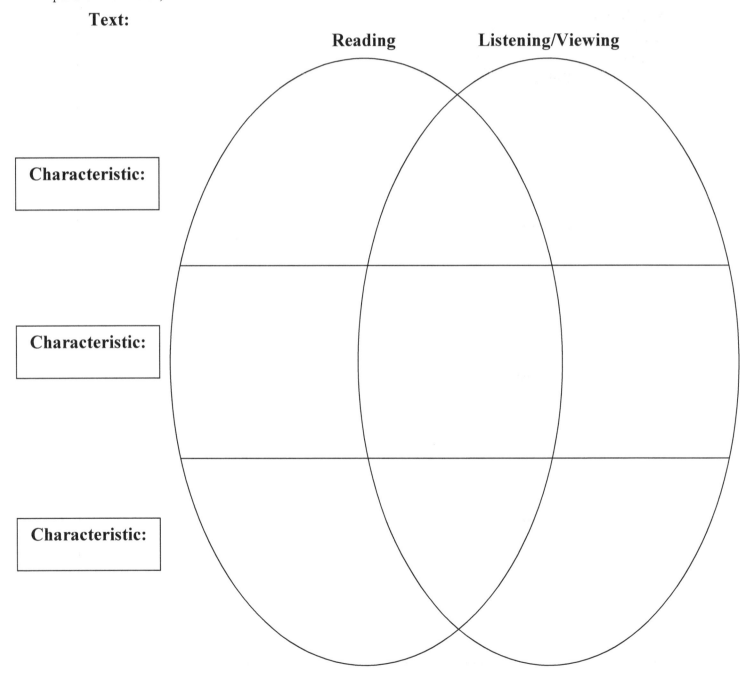

## CCSS.ELA-Literacy.RL.6.9

Compare and contrast texts in different forms or genres (e.g., stories and poems; historical novels and fantasy stories) in terms of their approaches to similar themes and topics.*

## Explanation

This standard asks students to note the similarities and differences of reading literature texts from different genres on related issues. With this graphic organizer, students are able to write the texts' name and form/genre at the top and identify the similar theme/topic of both texts' in the boxes on the left. Then, based on that theme/topic, differences are identified in the non-intersecting parts of the circles, and similarities are identified in the intersection of the two circles.

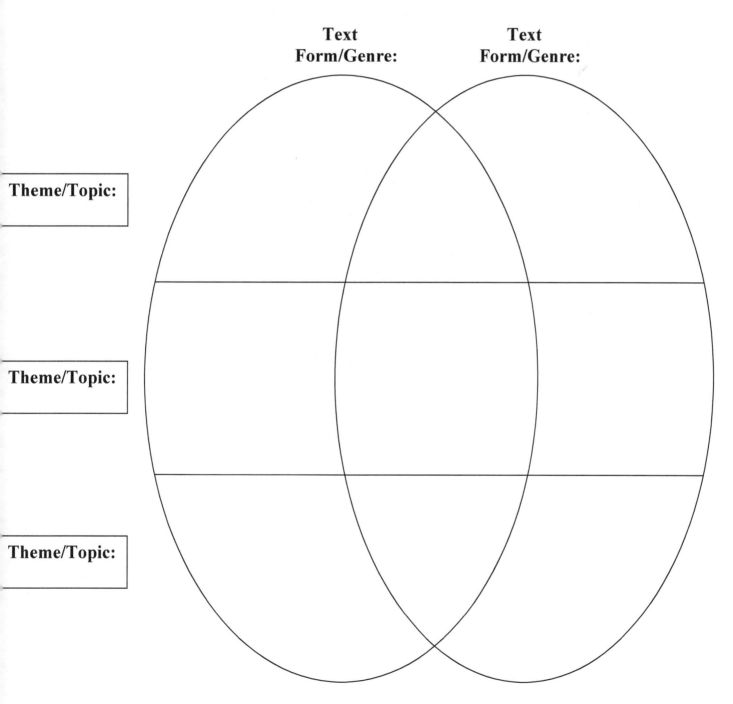

## <u>CCSS.ELA-Literacy.RL.6.10</u>

By the end of the year, read and comprehend literature, including stories, dramas, and poems, in the grades 6–8 text complexity band proficiently, with scaffolding as needed at the high end of the range.*

## <u>Explanation</u>

This standard asks students to read literature texts that are grade-level appropriate. No table or graphic organizer is applicable.

# CHAPTER 3

# 6th Grade Writing

# CCSS.ELA-Literacy.W.6.1

Write arguments to support claims with clear reasons and relevant evidence.*

# CCSS.ELA-Literacy.W.6.1.a

Introduce claim(s) and organize the reasons and evidence clearly.*

# CCSS.ELA-Literacy.W.6.1.b

Support claim(s) with clear reasons and relevant evidence, using credible sources and demonstrating an understanding of the topic or text.*

# Explanation

This group of standards asks students to write to persuade through the use of claims, sourced reasons, and sourced evidence. With this graphic organizer, students are able to brainstorm a claim in the top box and reasons, evidence, and sources in the bottom box.

**Claim**

|  |
|  |

↓

| Support | Support | Support |
|---|---|---|
| Reason 1- | Reason 2- | Reason 3- |
| Evidence 1- | Evidence 2- | Evidence 3- |
| Source- | Source- | Source- |
| Is it credible?- | Is it credible?- | Is it credible?- |

## CCSS.ELA-Literacy.W.6.1

Write arguments to support claims with clear reasons and relevant evidence.*

## CCSS.ELA-Literacy.W.6.1.c

Use words, phrases, and clauses to clarify the relationships among claim(s) and reasons.*

## Explanation

This standard asks students to use particular language to associate claim and reasons within persuasive writing. With this graphic organizer, students are able to write a claim in the left column, write reasons in the middle column, and brainstorm words, phrases, and/or clauses that clarify the relationship among them in the right column.

| Claim | Reasons | Words/Phrases/Clauses That Clarify |
|-------|---------|-----------------------------------|
|       | 1       |                                   |
|       | 2       |                                   |
|       | 3       |                                   |

## CCSS.ELA-Literacy.W.6.1

Write arguments to support claims with clear reasons and relevant evidence.*

## CCSS.ELA-Literacy.W.6.1.d

Establish and maintain a formal style.*

## Explanation

This standard asks students to have a formal writing style within persuasive writing. Because this standard leaves room for a teacher's interpretation, this example guide allows for modeling and guided practice so that students understand the difference between formal and informal writing styles.

## Informal Writing Style:

_____

_____

_____

_____

_____

_____

_____

## Formal Writing Style:

_____

_____

_____

_____

_____

_____

_____

## CCSS.ELA-Literacy.W.6.1

Write arguments to support claims with clear reasons and relevant evidence.*

## CCSS.ELA-Literacy.W.6.1.e

Provide a concluding statement or section that follows from the argument presented.*

## Explanation

This standard asks students to write a conclusion for persuasive writing. With this graphic organizer, students are able to write claims, reasons, and/or evidence in the top three boxes and, based on that, brainstorm a logical conclusion in the bottom box.

| Claim/Reason/ Evidence 1 | Claim/Reason/ Evidence 2 | Claim/Reason/ Evidence 3 |
| --- | --- | --- |
| | | |

**Conclusion**

## CCSS.ELA-Literacy.W.6.2

Write informative/explanatory texts to examine a topic and convey ideas, concepts, and information through the selection, organization, and analysis of relevant content.*

## CCSS.ELA-Literacy.W.6.2.a

Introduce a topic; organize ideas, concepts, and information, using strategies such as definition, classification, comparison/contrast, and cause/effect; include formatting (e.g., headings), graphics (e.g., charts, tables), and multimedia when useful to aiding comprehension.*

## Explanation

This standard asks students to utilize the elements of introduction, organization, formatting, and graphics/multimedia for informative/explanatory writing. With this graphic organizer, students are able to write the topic at the top and brainstorm an introduction in the first table, an organization strategy in the second table, formatting in the third table, and graphics/multimedia in the fourth table.

**Topic:**

| Introduction | |
|---|---|
| - | - |
| - | - |

| Organization Strategy<br>(Definition, Classification, Comparison/Contrast, and Cause/Effect) |
|---|
| |

| Formatting<br>(Headings) |
|---|
| |

| Graphics/Multimedia<br>(Charts, Tables) |
|---|
| |

## CCSS.ELA-Literacy.W.6.2

Write informative/explanatory texts to examine a topic and convey ideas, concepts, and information through the selection, organization, and analysis of relevant content.*

## CCSS.ELA-Literacy.W.6.2.b

Develop the topic with relevant facts, definitions, concrete details, quotations, or other information and examples.*

## Explanation

This standard asks students to use the micro elements of facts, definitions, details, quotations, and examples within informative/explanatory writing. With this graphic organizer, students are able to write the topic/issue at the top and brainstorm these elements below.

| Development |
|---|
| **Facts-** |
| **Definitions-** |
| **Concrete Details-** |
| **Quotations-** |
| **Other Information/Examples-** |

## CCSS.ELA-Literacy.W.6.2

Write informative/explanatory texts to examine a topic and convey ideas, concepts, and information through the selection, organization, and analysis of relevant content.*

## CCSS.ELA-Literacy.W.6.2.c

Use appropriate transitions to clarify the relationships among ideas and concepts.*

## Explanation

This standard asks students to use particular language to explain the association of ideas and concepts within informative/explanatory writing. With this graphic organizer, students are able to write ideas and concepts in the left table and brainstorm transitions that create cohesion and clarify how they relate in the right boxes.

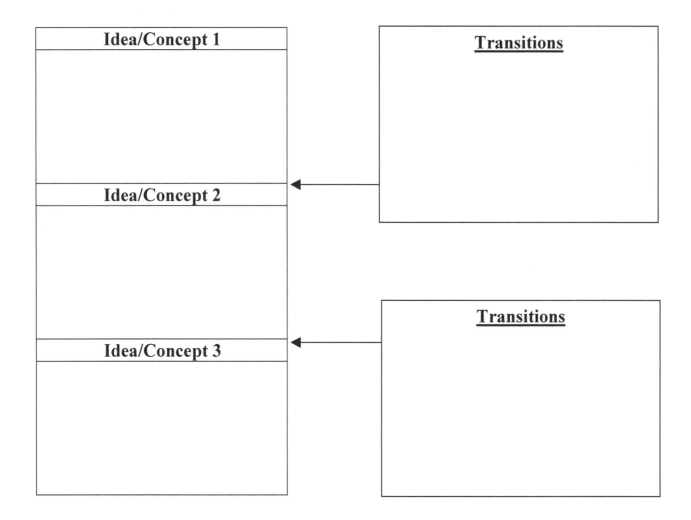

## CCSS.ELA-Literacy.W.6.2

Write informative/explanatory texts to examine a topic and convey ideas, concepts, and information through the selection, organization, and analysis of relevant content.*

## CCSS.ELA-Literacy.W.6.2.d

Use precise language and domain-specific vocabulary to inform about or explain the topic.*

## Explanation

This standard asks students to utilize certain subject matter words within informative/explanatory writing. With this graphic organizer, students are able to write the topic at the top and brainstorm precise domain-specific vocabulary that relates to the topic below.

### Topic:

| Precise/Domain-Specific Vocabulary |
| --- |
|  |

## CCSS.ELA-Literacy.W.6.2

Write informative/explanatory texts to examine a topic and convey ideas, concepts, and information through the selection, organization, and analysis of relevant content.*

## CCSS.ELA-Literacy.W.6.2.e

Establish and maintain a formal style.*

## Explanation

This standard asks students to have a formal writing style within informative/explanatory writing. Because this standard leaves room for a teacher's interpretation, this example guide allows for modeling and guided practice so that students understand the difference between formal and informal writing styles.

## Informal Writing Style:

_____

_____

_____

_____

_____

_____

_____

_____

## Formal Writing Style:

_____

_____

_____

_____

_____

_____

_____

_____

## CCSS.ELA-Literacy.W.6.2

Write informative/explanatory texts to examine a topic and convey ideas, concepts, and information through the selection, organization, and analysis of relevant content.*

## CCSS.ELA-Literacy.W.6.2.f

Provide a concluding statement or section that follows from the information or explanation presented.*

## Explanation

This standard asks students to write a conclusion for informative/explanatory writing. With this graphic organizer, students are able to write concepts or ideas presented in the top three boxes and, based on that, brainstorm a logical conclusion in the bottom box.

| Concept/Idea 1 | Concept/Idea 2 | Concept/Idea 3 |
|---|---|---|
| | | |

**Conclusion**

## CCSS.ELA-Literacy.W.6.3

Write narratives to develop real or imagined experiences or events using effective technique, relevant descriptive details, and well-structured event sequences.*

## CCSS.ELA-Literacy.W.6.3.a

Engage and orient the reader by establishing a context and introducing a narrator and/or characters; organize an event sequence that unfolds naturally and logically.*

## CCSS.ELA-Literacy.W.6.3.b

Use narrative techniques, such as dialogue, pacing, and description, to develop experiences, events, and/or characters.*

## CCSS.ELA-Literacy.W.6.3.d

Use precise words and phrases, relevant descriptive details, and sensory language to convey experiences and events.*

## Explanation

This group of standards asks students to have the macro elements of context, characters, and event sequence and micro elements of dialogue, pacing, description, precise language, relevant descriptive details, and sensory language that develop experiences, events, and/or characters in narrative writing. With this graphic organizer, students are able to brainstorm these elements, making sure they relate to each other.

### Establish

| |
|---|
| **Context:** |
| **Characters/Narrator:** |

### Event Sequence

| Event 1 | **Narrative Technique (Choose):**<br>Dialogue, Pacing, or Description | **To Develop (Choose):** |
|---|---|---|
| | precise words and phrases, relevant descriptive details, and sensory language: | Events, Characters, or Experiences |

*Continued on next page

| Event 2 | **Narrative Technique (Choose):** Dialogue, Pacing, or Description | **To Develop (Choose):** |
|---|---|---|
| | precise words and phrases, relevant descriptive details, and sensory language: | Events, Characters, or Experiences |

| Event 3 | **Narrative Technique (Choose):** Dialogue, Pacing, or Description | **To Develop (Choose):** |
|---|---|---|
| | precise words and phrases, relevant descriptive details, and sensory language: | Events, Characters, or Experiences |

| Event 4 | **Narrative Technique (Choose):** Dialogue, Pacing, or Description | **To Develop (Choose):** |
|---|---|---|
| | precise words and phrases, relevant descriptive details, and sensory language: | Events, Characters, or Experiences |

| Event 5 | **Narrative Technique (Choose):** Dialogue, Pacing, or Description | **To Develop (Choose):** |
|---|---|---|
| | precise words and phrases, relevant descriptive details, and sensory language: | Events, Characters, or Experiences |

## CCSS.ELA-Literacy.W.6.3

Write narratives to develop real or imagined experiences or events using effective technique, relevant descriptive details, and well-structured event sequences.*

## CCSS.ELA-Literacy.W.6.3.c

Use a variety of transition words, phrases, and clauses to convey sequence and signal shifts from one time frame or setting to another.*

## Explanation

This standard asks students to use particular language to express time progression within narrative writing. With this graphic organizer, students are able to write events in the left table and brainstorm words, phrases, and clauses that convey sequence and signal shifts from one time frame or setting to another in the right boxes.

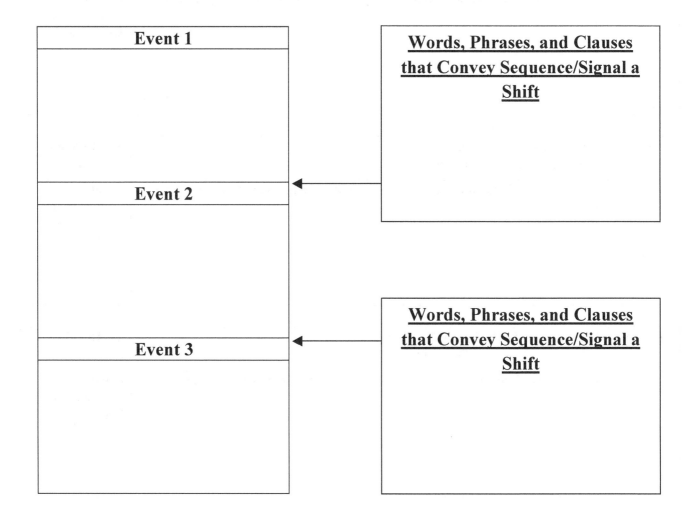

## CCSS.ELA-Literacy.W.6.3

Write narratives to develop real or imagined experiences or events using effective technique, relevant descriptive details, and well-structured event sequences.*

## CCSS.ELA-Literacy.W.6.3.e

Provide a conclusion that follows from the narrated experiences or events.*

## Explanation

This standard asks students to write a conclusion for narrative writing. With this graphic organizer, students are able to write experiences or events of the narrative in the top three boxes and, based on that, brainstorm a logical conclusion in the bottom box.

| Event/Experience 1 | Event/Experience 2 | Event/Experience 3 |
| --- | --- | --- |
| | | |

**Conclusion**

# CCSS.ELA-Literacy.W.6.4

Produce clear and coherent writing in which the development, organization, and style are appropriate to task, purpose, and audience. (Grade-specific expectations for writing types are defined in standards 1–3 above.)*

## Explanation

This standard asks students to have clear/coherent writing for persuasive, informative/explanatory, and narrative texts. Because this standard leaves room for a teacher's interpretation, this example guide allows for modeling and guided practice so that students understand the difference between unclear/incoherent and clear/coherent writing styles.

## Unclear/Incoherent Writing Style:

_____

_____

_____

_____

_____

_____

_____

## Clear/Coherent Writing Style:

_____

_____

_____

_____

_____

_____

_____

## CCSS.ELA-Literacy.W.6.5

With some guidance and support from peers and adults, develop and strengthen writing as needed by planning, revising, editing, rewriting, or trying a new approach. (Editing for conventions should demonstrate command of Language standards 1–3 up to and including grade 6 here.)*

## Explanation

This standard asks students to use the writing process for persuasive, informative/explanatory, and narrative texts. No table or graphic organizer is applicable.

## <u>CCSS.ELA-Literacy.W.6.6</u>

Use technology, including the Internet, to produce and publish writing as well as to interact and collaborate with others; demonstrate sufficient command of keyboarding skills to type a minimum of three pages in a single sitting.*

## <u>Explanation</u>

This standard asks students to use technology for persuasive, informative/explanatory, and narrative texts. No table or graphic organizer is applicable.

# CCSS.ELA-Literacy.W.6.7

Conduct short research projects to answer a question, drawing on several sources and refocusing the inquiry when appropriate.*

## Explanation

This standard asks students to find information from sources for research writing and refine the query if appropriate. With this graphic organizer, students are able to write their research question at the top, identify information from various sources in the boxes, make sure it is related to their research question at the top, and consider refocusing when appropriate.

**Research Question-** _____

| **Source #1/Findings** | **Source #2/Findings** |
|---|---|

Is a refocus needed?                    Is a refocus needed?

**Source #3/Findings**

Is a refocus needed?

## CCSS.ELA-Literacy.W.6.8

Gather relevant information from multiple print and digital sources; assess the credibility of each source; and quote or paraphrase the data and conclusions of others while avoiding plagiarism and providing basic bibliographic information for sources.*

## Explanation

This standard asks students to find pertinent information, evaluate the value of the information, quote/paraphrase the information without plagiarism, and cite sources. With this graphic organizer, students are able to write the research question at the top, quote and/or paraphrase findings in the second column, cite sources in the third column, and assess the credibility of those sources in the fourth column.

### Research Question-_____

| | Findings | Sources in Bibliographical Form | Source Credibility |
|---|---|---|---|
| **Quote** | | | |
| **Paraphrase** | | | |

## CCSS.ELA-Literacy.W.6.9

Draw evidence from literary or informational texts to support analysis, reflection, and research.*

## CCSS.ELA-Literacy.W.6.9.a

Apply *grade 6 Reading standards* to literature (e.g., "Compare and contrast texts in different forms or genres [e.g., stories and poems; historical novels and fantasy stories] in terms of their approaches to similar themes and topics").*

## CCSS.ELA-Literacy.W.6.9.b

Apply *grade 6 Reading standards* to literary nonfiction (e.g., "Trace and evaluate the argument and specific claims in a text, distinguishing claims that are supported by reasons and evidence from claims that are not").*

## Explanation

This group of standards asks students to write for the purpose of expressing the reading standards. With the first example guide, students are able to link a literature reading standard at the top to related analysis, reflection, and research below it. With the second example guide, students are able to link a literary nonfiction reading standard at the top to related analysis, reflection, and research below it.

**Literature Standard:**_____

**Analysis/Reflection/Research:**

_____

_____

_____

_____

_____

**Literary Nonfiction Standard:**_____

**Analysis/Reflection/Research:**

_____

_____

_____

_____

_____

## CCSS.ELA-Literacy.W.6.10

Write routinely over extended time frames (time for research, reflection, and revision) and shorter time frames (a single sitting or a day or two) for a range of discipline-specific tasks, purposes, and audiences.*

## Explanation

This standard asks students to write short and long pieces of writing. No table or graphic organizer is applicable.

# CHAPTER 4

# 6th Grade
# Speaking/Listening

## CCSS.ELA-Literacy.SL.6.1

Engage effectively in a range of collaborative discussions (one-on-one, in groups, and teacher-led) with diverse partners on grade 6 topics, texts, and issues, building on others' ideas and expressing their own clearly.*

## CCSS.ELA-Literacy.SL.6.1.a

Come to discussions prepared, having read or studied required material; explicitly draw on that preparation by referring to evidence on the topic, text, or issue to probe and reflect on ideas under discussion.*

## Explanation

This standard asks students to be ready with topical evidence for class discussions. With this graphic organizer, students are able to write the topic/text/issue at the top and prepare using an outline, a graphic organizer, or both.

### Topic/Text/Issue of Discussion:

| Evidence From Reading/Studying: | Evidence From Reading/Studying: |
|---|---|
| I.<br>A.<br>B.<br>C.<br><br>II.<br>A.<br>B.<br>C.<br><br>III.<br>A.<br>B.<br>C.<br><br>IV.<br>A.<br>B.<br>C.<br><br>V.<br>A.<br>B.<br>C. | |

## CCSS.ELA-Literacy.SL.6.1

Engage effectively in a range of collaborative discussions (one-on-one, in groups, and teacher-led) with diverse partners on grade 6 topics, texts, and issues, building on others' ideas and expressing their own clearly.*

## CCSS.ELA-Literacy.SL.6.1.b

Follow rules for collegial discussions, set specific goals and deadlines, and define individual roles as needed.*

## Explanation

This standard asks students to participate in setting class discussion norms. With this graphic organizer, students are able to write the topic/issue at the top and propose rules, goals, deadlines, and roles in the second column.

### Topic/Issue of Discussion:

| Rules | |
|---|---|
| **Goals** | |
| **Deadlines** | |
| **Individual Roles** | |

## CCSS.ELA-Literacy.SL.6.1

Engage effectively in a range of collaborative discussions (one-on-one, in groups, and teacher-led) with diverse partners on grade 6 topics, texts, and issues, building on others' ideas and expressing their own clearly.*

## CCSS.ELA-Literacy.SL.6.1.c

Pose and respond to specific questions with elaboration and detail by making comments that contribute to the topic, text, or issue under discussion.*

## Explanation

This standard asks students to participate in class discussion with comments and questions. With this graphic organizer, students are able to write the topic/text/issue at the top, comments in the first table, and questions in the second table.

## Topic/Text/Issue of Discussion:

| Comments (That contribute to the topic, text, or issue): |
|---|
| |

| Questions: |
|---|
| |

## CCSS.ELA-Literacy.SL.6.1

Engage effectively in a range of collaborative discussions (one-on-one, in groups, and teacher-led) with diverse partners on grade 6 topics, texts, and issues, building on others' ideas and expressing their own clearly.*

## CCSS.ELA-Literacy.SL.6.1.d

Review the key ideas expressed and demonstrate understanding of multiple perspectives through reflection and paraphrasing.*

## Explanation

This standard asks students to report thoughts and perspectives given in class discussions. With this graphic organizer, students are able to write the topic/issue at the top and review key ideas using an outline, a graphic organizer, or both.

**Topic/Issue of Discussion:**

| **Review of Key Ideas:** | **Review of Key Ideas:** |
|---|---|
| Perspective I:<br>A.<br>B.<br>C.<br><br>Perspective II:<br>A.<br>B.<br>C.<br><br>Perspective III:<br>A.<br>B.<br>C.<br><br>Perspective IV:<br>A.<br>B.<br>C.<br><br>Perspective V:<br>A.<br>B.<br>C. | Perspective 1<br><br>Perspective 2<br><br>Perspective 3 |

# CCSS.ELA-Literacy.SL.6.2

Interpret information presented in diverse media and formats (e.g., visually, quantitatively, orally) and explain how it contributes to a topic, text, or issue under study.*

## Explanation

This standard asks students to infer and detail the contribution of various types of given material. With this graphic organizer, students are able to write the topic, text, or issue at the top, interpret the information presented in the left column, and explain how it contributes to the topic, text, or issue under study in the right column.

### Topic/Text/Issue:

| Interpretation | Contribution Explanation |
|---|---|
| **Visual Information:** | |
| **Quantitative Information:** | |
| **Oral Information:** | |

## CCSS.ELA-Literacy.SL.6.3

Delineate a speaker's argument and specific claims, distinguishing claims that are supported by reasons and evidence from claims that are not.*

## Explanation

This standard asks students to dissect a speaker's argument or claim in terms of reasons and evidence, then assess which claims are supported and which claims are not. With this graphic organizer, if the argument or claim can be supported, then the claim is written in the top left box and the reasons/evidence are written in the left column. If the argument or claim can't be supported, then the claim is written in the top right box and the reasons/evidence are written in the right column.

| **Argument/Claim** | **Argument/Claim** |
| --- | --- |

| **Supporting Reasons/Evidence** | **Unsupported Reasons/Evidence** |
| --- | --- |
| Reasons- | Reasons- |
| Evidence- | Evidence- |

## CCSS.ELA-Literacy.SL.6.4

Present claims and findings, sequencing ideas logically and using pertinent descriptions, facts, and details to accentuate main ideas or themes; use appropriate eye contact, adequate volume, and clear pronunciation.*

## Explanation

This standard asks students to be ready for class speeches with proper topic chronology, explanations, and data. With this graphic organizer, students are able to write the finding/claim at the top and express these elements using an outline, a graphic organizer, or both.

**Finding/Claim:**

| Descriptions, Facts, Details: | Descriptions, Facts, Details: |
|---|---|
| I. <br> A. <br> B. <br> C. <br><br> II. <br> A. <br> B. <br> C. <br><br> III. <br> A. <br> B. <br> C. <br><br> IV. <br> A. <br> B. <br> C. <br><br> V. <br> A. <br> B. <br> C. | |

# CCSS.ELA-Literacy.SL.6.5

Include multimedia components (e.g., graphics, images, music, sound) and visual displays in presentations to clarify information.*

## Explanation

This standard asks students to be ready for class speeches using interactive media elements and visuals. With this graphic organizer, students are able to brainstorm what they intend to present in the left column and relate what multimedia and visuals could be utilized in their speeches in the right column.

| Presentation Information (Main Ideas) | Possible Multimedia Components (Graphics, Images, Music, Sound)/Visuals |
|---|---|
| | |
| | |
| | |
| | |

## CCSS.ELA-Literacy.SL.6.6

Adapt speech to a variety of contexts and tasks, demonstrating command of formal English when indicated or appropriate. (See grade 6 Language standards 1 and 3 for specific expectations.)*

## Explanation

This standard asks students to speak within a range of grade-level situations. No table or graphic organizer is applicable.

# CHAPTER 5

# 6th Grade Language

## CCSS.ELA-Literacy.L.6.1

Demonstrate command of the conventions of standard English grammar and usage when writing or speaking.*

## CCSS.ELA-Literacy.L.6.1.a

Ensure that pronouns are in the proper case (subjective, objective, possessive).*

## Explanation

This standard asks students to use subjective, objective, possessive pronouns correctly. With this table and example guide, students are given the pronouns at the top and space to write paragraphs and/or sentences using them at the bottom.

| Subject | | Object | | Possessive |
|---|---|---|---|---|
| I | = | me | = | mine |
| you | = | you | = | yours |
| he | = | him | = | his |
| she | = | her | = | hers |
| it | = | it | = | its |
| we | = | us | = | ours |
| they | = | them | = | theirs |

_____

_____

_____

_____

_____

_____

_____

## CCSS.ELA-Literacy.L.6.1

Demonstrate command of the conventions of standard English grammar and usage when writing or speaking.*

## CCSS.ELA-Literacy.L.6.1.b

Use intensive pronouns (e.g., *myself, ourselves*).*

## Explanation

This standard asks students to utilize intensive pronouns. With this example guide, students are given the intensive pronouns and space to use them in sentences.

**myself:**

_____

**yourself:**

_____

**himself:**

_____

**herself:**

_____

**itself:**

_____

**ourselves:**

_____

**themselves:**

_____

## CCSS.ELA-Literacy.L.6.1

Demonstrate command of the conventions of standard English grammar and usage when writing or speaking.*

## CCSS.ELA-Literacy.L.6.1c

Recognize and correct inappropriate shifts in pronoun number and person.*

## Explanation

This standard asks students to notice mistakes with pronoun shift and rectify them. With this example guide, students are given space to discern the difference between appropriate and inappropriate pronoun shifts.

**Inappropriate Pronoun Shift:**

_____

**Appropriate Pronoun Shift:**

_____

**Inappropriate Pronoun Shift:**

_____

**Appropriate Pronoun Shift:**

_____

**Inappropriate Pronoun Shift:**

_____

**Appropriate Pronoun Shift:**

_____

**Inappropriate Pronoun Shift:**

_____

**Appropriate Pronoun Shift:**

_____

## CCSS.ELA-Literacy.L.6.1

Demonstrate command of the conventions of standard English grammar and usage when writing or speaking.*

## CCSS.ELA-Literacy.L.6.1.d

Recognize and correct vague pronouns (i.e., ones with unclear or ambiguous antecedents).*

## Explanation

This standard asks students to notice mistakes with vague pronouns and rectify them. With this example guide, students are given space to discern the difference between vague and clear pronoun use.

**Vague:**

_____

**Corrected/Clear:**

_____

**Vague:**

_____

**Corrected/Clear:**

_____

**Vague:**

_____

**Corrected/Clear:**

_____

**Vague:**

_____

**Corrected/Clear:**

_____

# CCSS.ELA-Literacy.L.6.1

Demonstrate command of the conventions of standard English grammar and usage when writing or speaking.*

# CCSS.ELA-Literacy.L.6.1.e

Recognize variations from standard English in their own and others' writing and speaking, and identify and use strategies to improve expression in conventional language.*

# Explanation

This standard asks students to notice differences between standard and non-standard English as well as strategies for enhancement. With this example guide, students are given space to discern the difference between the two types of language use and list improvement strategies at the bottom.

## Variation:

_____

## Standard:

_____

## Variation:

_____

## Standard:

_____

## Variation:

_____

## Standard:

_____

## Strategies to Improve Expression in Conventional Language:

- 

- 

-

# CCSS.ELA-Literacy.L.6.2

Demonstrate command of the conventions of standard English capitalization, punctuation, and spelling when writing.*

# CCSS.ELA-Literacy.L.6.2.a

Use punctuation (commas, parentheses, dashes) to set off nonrestrictive/parenthetical elements.*

# Explanation

This standard asks students to utilize commas, parentheses, and dashes to separate nonrestrictive/parenthetical parts of sentences. With this example guide, students are given space to discern the difference between the three types of punctuation that can be used to set off nonrestrictive/parenthetical sentence elements.

**Commas:**

_____

**Parentheses:**

_____

**Dashes:**

_____

**Commas:**

_____

**Parentheses:**

_____

**Dashes:**

_____

**Commas:**

_____

**Parentheses:**

_____

**Dashes:**

_____

## CCSS.ELA-Literacy.L.6.2

Demonstrate command of the conventions of standard English capitalization, punctuation, and spelling when writing.*

## CCSS.ELA-Literacy.L.6.2.b

Spell correctly.*

## Explanation

This standard asks students to spell words precisely. No table or graphic organizer is applicable.

## CCSS.ELA-Literacy.L.6.3

Use knowledge of language and its conventions when writing, speaking, reading, or listening.*

## CCSS.ELA-Literacy.L.6.3.a

Vary sentence patterns for meaning, reader/listener interest, and style.*

## Explanation

This standard asks students to strategically utilize different types of sentences. With this example guide, students are given space to discern the difference among seven sentence patterns.

**Simple Sentence:**

_____

**Compound Sentence:**

_____

**Exclamatory Sentence:**

_____

**Complex Sentence:**

_____

**Interrogative Sentence:**

_____

**Imperative Sentence:**

_____

**Conditional Sentence:**

_____

## CCSS.ELA-Literacy.L.6.3

Use knowledge of language and its conventions when writing, speaking, reading, or listening.*

## CCSS.ELA-Literacy.L.6.3.b

Maintain consistency in style and tone.*

## Explanation

This standard asks students to sustain a uniform language style and tone. Because this standard leaves room for a teacher's interpretation, this example guide allows for modeling and guided practice so that students understand the difference between inconsistent style/tone and consistent style/tone.

## Inconsistent Style/Tone:

_____

_____

_____

_____

_____

_____

_____

## Consistent Style/Tone:

_____

_____

_____

_____

_____

_____

_____

_____

## CCSS.ELA-Literacy.L.6.4

Determine or clarify the meaning of unknown and multiple-meaning words and phrases based on grade 6 reading and content, choosing flexibly from a range of strategies.*

## CCSS.ELA-Literacy.L.6.4.a

Use context (e.g., the overall meaning of a sentence or paragraph; a word's position or function in a sentence) as a clue to the meaning of a word or phrase.*

## Explanation

This standard asks students to utilize context for word definition clues. With this graphic organizer, students are able to write the unknown word or phrase in the left column, relate given clues to its meaning in the middle column, and make an educated guess about its definition in the right column.

| Unknown Word/Phrase | Possible Clue Words/ Overall Meaning/ Position or Function | Possible Meaning of Unknown Word/Phrase |
|---|---|---|
|  |  |  |
|  |  |  |
|  |  |  |
|  |  |  |
|  |  |  |
|  |  |  |
|  |  |  |

*The Visual Edge©*

## CCSS.ELA-Literacy.L.6.4

Determine or clarify the meaning of unknown and multiple-meaning words and phrases based on grade 6 reading and content, choosing flexibly from a range of strategies.*

## CCSS.ELA-Literacy.L.6.4.b

Use common, grade-appropriate Greek or Latin affixes and roots as clues to the meaning of a word (e.g., *audience, auditory, audible*).*

## Explanation

This standard asks students to utilize affixes/roots as word definition clues. With this graphic organizer, students are able to use the first table to identify affixes/roots in the first and third columns and write definitions next to each. Students are able to use the second table to write an unknown word in the left column, pick out its affix/root in the middle column, and based on the affix/root definition from the first table, make an educated guess about the unknown word's definition in the right column.

| 6th Grade Affix/Root | Definition | 6th Grade Affix/Root | Definition |
|---|---|---|---|
| | | | |
| | | | |
| | | | |
| | | | |
| | | | |
| | | | |
| | | | |
| | | | |
| | | | |
| | | | |
| | | | |

| Unknown Word | Affix/Root | Possible Definition of Unknown Word |
|---|---|---|
| | | |
| | | |
| | | |
| | | |

## CCSS.ELA-Literacy.L.6.4

Determine or clarify the meaning of unknown and multiple-meaning words and phrases based on grade 6 reading and content, choosing flexibly from a range of strategies.*

## CCSS.ELA-Literacy.L.6.4.c

Consult reference materials (e.g., dictionaries, glossaries, thesauruses), both print and digital, to find the pronunciation of a word or determine or clarify its precise meaning or its part of speech.*

## Explanation

This standard asks students to utilize reference resources for unknown words. With this graphic organizer, students are able to write the unknown word in the left column and relate its pronunciation, definition, or part of speech from a reference material in the right column.

| Unknown Word | Reference Material-Definition/Part of Speech/Pronunciation |
|---|---|
|  |  |
|  |  |
|  |  |
|  |  |
|  |  |
|  |  |
|  |  |
|  |  |
|  |  |
|  |  |
|  |  |
|  |  |
|  |  |
|  |  |

## CCSS.ELA-Literacy.L.6.4

Determine or clarify the meaning of unknown and multiple-meaning words and phrases based on grade 6 reading and content, choosing flexibly from a range of strategies.*

## CCSS.ELA-Literacy.L.6.4.d

Verify the preliminary determination of the meaning of a word or phrase (e.g., by checking the inferred meaning in context or in a dictionary).*

## Explanation

This standard asks students to utilize context and dictionaries for word definition confirmation. With this graphic organizer, students are able to write the unknown word or phrase in the left column, relate its preliminary meaning in the middle column, and verify the definition in the right column.

| Word/Phrase | Preliminary Determination of Meaning | Inferred Meaning in Context/Dictionary |
|---|---|---|
|  |  |  |
|  |  |  |
|  |  |  |
|  |  |  |
|  |  |  |
|  |  |  |
|  |  |  |
|  |  |  |
|  |  |  |
|  |  |  |
|  |  |  |
|  |  |  |
|  |  |  |

## CCSS.ELA-Literacy.L.6.5

Demonstrate understanding of figurative language, word relationships, and nuances in word meanings.*

## CCSS.ELA-Literacy.L.6.5.a

Interpret figures of speech (e.g., personification) in context.*

## Explanation

This standard asks students to explain figures of speech. With this graphic organizer, students are able to write the figure of speech in the top row and interpret it in the bottom row.

| **Figure of Speech**<br>(Personification) | | | |
|---|---|---|---|
| **Interpretation** | | | |

## CCSS.ELA-Literacy.L.6.5

Demonstrate understanding of figurative language, word relationships, and nuances in word meanings.*

## CCSS.ELA-Literacy.L.6.5.b

Use the relationship between particular words (e.g., cause/effect, part/whole, item/category) to better understand each of the words.*

## Explanation

This standard asks students to utilize word relationships as clues to their meaning. With this graphic organizer, students are able to write two associated words in columns one and two based on the relationship stated in the third column and explain the two associated words in the fourth column.

| Word 1 | Word 2 | Relationship | Explanation |
|--------|--------|--------------|-------------|
| **Word 1** | **Word 2** | **Relationship** <br><br> cause/effect | **Explanation** <br> 1- <br><br> 2- |
| **Word 1** | **Word 2** | **Relationship** <br><br> object/function | **Explanation** <br> 1- <br><br> 2- |
| **Word 1** | **Word 2** | **Relationship** <br><br> item/category | **Explanation** <br> 1- <br><br> 2- |
| **Word 1** | **Word 2** | **Relationship** <br><br> synonym | **Explanation** <br> 1- <br><br> 2- |
| **Word 1** | **Word 2** | **Relationship** <br><br> antonym | **Explanation** <br> 1- <br><br> 2- |
| **Word 1** | **Word 2** | **Relationship** <br><br> part/whole | **Explanation** <br> 1- <br><br> 2- |

## CCSS.ELA-Literacy.L.6.5

Demonstrate understanding of figurative language, word relationships, and nuances in word meanings.*

## CCSS.ELA-Literacy.L.6.5.c

Distinguish among the connotations (associations) of words with similar denotations (definitions) (e.g., *stingy, scrimping, economical, unwasteful, thrifty*).*

## Explanation

This standard asks students to notice the differences between the connotations and denotations of a group of words. With this graphic organizer, students are able to write similar words in the top row, relate their similar denotations in the middle row, and determine each word's connotation in the bottom row.

| Similar Words | | | |
| --- | --- | --- | --- |
| Denotation | | | |
| Connotation | | | |

| Similar Words | | | |
| --- | --- | --- | --- |
| Denotation | | | |
| Connotation | | | |

| Similar Words | | | |
| --- | --- | --- | --- |
| Denotation | | | |
| Connotation | | | |

## CCSS.ELA-Literacy.L.6.6

Acquire and use accurately grade-appropriate general academic and domain-specific words and phrases; gather vocabulary knowledge when considering a word or phrase important to comprehension or expression.*

## Explanation

This standard asks students to use vocabulary that is grade-level appropriate and collect vocabulary information. For the former, no table or graphic organizer is applicable, and the latter is addressed in CCSS.ELA-Literacy.L.6.4.

# Section 2

7th Grade

Graphic Organizers

CHAPTER 6

# 7th Grade
# Reading Informational Text

## CCSS.ELA-Literacy.RI.7.1

Cite several pieces of textual evidence to support analysis of what the text says explicitly as well as inferences drawn from the text.*

## Explanation

This standard asks students to indicate multiple pieces of proof of explicit and inferential meaning in an informational text. With this graphic organizer, students are able to analyze for explicit and inferential meaning in the top row and relate various pieces of evidence for those individual meanings in the bottom row.

| Explicit Meaning | |
|---|---|
| **Textual Evidence** | -<br><br>-<br><br>- |

| Inferential Meaning | |
|---|---|
| **Textual Evidence** | -<br><br>-<br><br>- |

## CCSS.ELA-Literacy.RI.7.2

Determine two or more central ideas in a text and analyze their development over the course of the text; provide an objective summary of the text.*

## Explanation

This standard asks students to establish two or more essential ideas and how they progress within an informational text, then summarize. With this graphic organizer, students are able to express the central ideas in the big boxes at the top and relate how they develop over the course of the text in the small boxes. Space is provided for a summary as well.

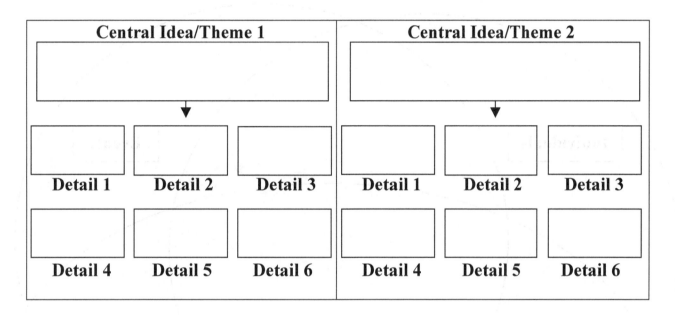

## Summary:

_____

_____

_____

_____

_____

_____

_____

_____

## CCSS.ELA-Literacy.RI.7.3

Analyze the interactions between individuals, events, and ideas in a text (e.g., how ideas influence individuals or events, or how individuals influence ideas or events).*

## Explanation

This standard asks students to examine how an informational text's individuals, events, and ideas relate. With this graphic organizer, students are able to use the intersecting segments of the circles to document how the different elements interact with/influence each other.

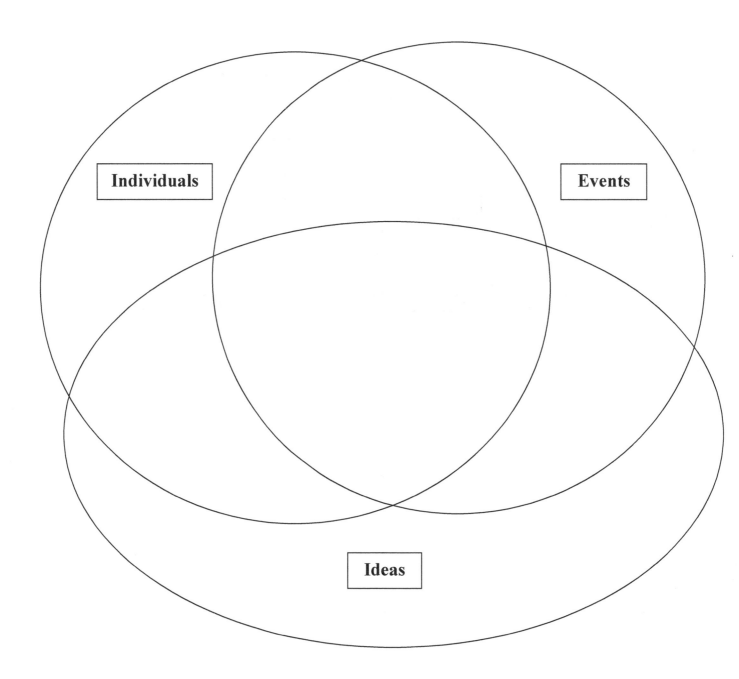

# CCSS.ELA-Literacy.RI.7.4

Determine the meaning of words and phrases as they are used in a text, including figurative, connotative, and technical meanings; analyze the impact of a specific word choice on meaning and tone.*

## Explanation

This standard asks students to establish different meanings for words and phrases in an informational text and determine the relationship of word choice to meaning and tone. With this graphic organizer, students are able to use the left table to write a word or phrase in the first column and describe its various definitions in the second column. Students are able to use the right table to write a specific word choice in the first column and analyze its impact on meaning and tone in the second column.

| Word/ Phrase | Definition |
|---|---|
|  | Figurative- <br><br><br><br> Connotative- <br><br><br><br> Technical- |

| Specific Word Choice | Impact Analysis |
|---|---|
|  | Meaning- <br><br><br><br> Tone- |

## CCSS.ELA-Literacy.RI.7.5

Analyze the structure an author uses to organize a text, including how the major sections contribute to the whole and to the development of the ideas.*

## Explanation

This standard asks students to determine how the structure of an informational text influences its holistic and topic development. With this graphic organizer, students are able to determine the text structure at the top, identify major text sections in the first table, and explain how those major sections contribute to the whole and to an understanding of the ideas in the second table.

**Text Structure (Choose One: Chronological/Sequence, Cause/Effect, Problem/Solution, Compare/Contrast, Description, or Directions):**

| Major Section 1 | Major Section 2 | Major Section 3 | Major Section 4 |
| --- | --- | --- | --- |
|  |  |  |  |

| Contribution to Whole | Contribution to Understanding of the Ideas |
| --- | --- |
|  |  |

# CCSS.ELA-Literacy.RI.7.6

Determine an author's point of view or purpose in a text and analyze how the author distinguishes his or her position from that of others.*

## Explanation

This standard asks students to establish an author's point of view or purpose in an informational text and examine how it is different from those of others. With this graphic organizer, students are able to write the author's point of view or purpose in the left column, relate his/her position in the middle column, and relate the position of others in the right column.

| Author's Point of View/ Purpose | Author's Position | Other's Position |
|---|---|---|
|  |  |  |

## CCSS.ELA-Literacy.RI.7.7

Compare and contrast a text to an audio, video, or multimedia version of the text, analyzing each medium's portrayal of the subject (e.g., how the delivery of a speech affects the impact of the words).*

## Explanation

This standard asks students to note the similarities and differences of an informational text to its audio, video, or multimedia version on the same subject. With this graphic organizer, students are able to write the name of the work at the top and identify the subject of both versions in the boxes on the left. Then, based on that subject, differences are identified in the non-intersecting parts of the circles, and similarities are identified in the intersection of the two circles.

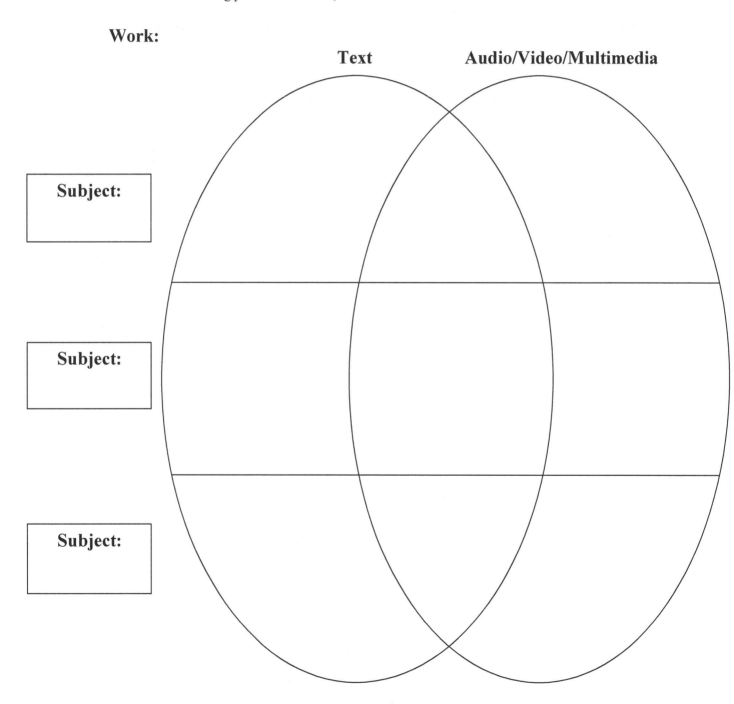

# CCSS.ELA-Literacy.RI.7.8

Trace and evaluate the argument and specific claims in a text, assessing whether the reasoning is sound and the evidence is relevant and sufficient to support the claims.*

## Explanation

This standard asks students to outline and assess an informational author's argument or claim in terms of reasons and evidence. With this graphic organizer, students are able to write the author's argument or claim in the top box, trace reasons and evidence for that claim in the left column, and evaluate reasons and evidence in the right column.

## Argument/Claim

| Trace | Evaluation |
|---|---|
| Reasons- | Soundness of Reasons- |
| Evidence- | Relevancy/Sufficiency of Evidence- |

## CCSS.ELA-Literacy.RI.7.9

Analyze how two or more authors writing about the same topic shape their presentations of key information by emphasizing different evidence or advancing different interpretations of facts.*

## Explanation

This standard asks students to examine the different approaches of two informational authors who write on the same subject, yet use varying proof and fact analysis. With this graphic organizer, students are able to write the topic at the top and author's names in the first row of each table and analyze each author's evidence emphasis in the first table and fact interpretation in the second table.

### Topic:

| | Author 1: | Author 2: |
|---|---|---|
| **Evidence Emphasis** | | |

| | Author 1: | Author 2: |
|---|---|---|
| **Fact Interpretation** | | |

## CCSS.ELA-Literacy.RI.7.10

By the end of the year, read and comprehend literary nonfiction in the grades 6–8 text complexity band proficiently, with scaffolding as needed at the high end of the range.*

## Explanation

This standard asks students to read nonfiction texts that are grade-level appropriate. No table or graphic organizer is applicable.

CHAPTER 7

# 7th Grade
# Reading Literature Text

## CCSS.ELA-Literacy.RL.7.1

Cite several pieces of textual evidence to support analysis of what the text says explicitly as well as inferences drawn from the text.*

## Explanation

This standard asks students to indicate multiple pieces of proof of explicit and inferential meaning within a literature text. With this graphic organizer, students are able to analyze for explicit and inferential meaning in the top row and relate various pieces of evidence for those individual meanings in the bottom row.

| Explicit Meaning | |
|---|---|
| Textual Evidence | -<br><br>-<br><br>- |

| Inferential Meaning | |
|---|---|
| Textual Evidence | -<br><br>-<br><br>- |

## CCSS.ELA-Literacy.RL.7.2

Determine a theme or central idea of a text and analyze its development over the course of the text; provide an objective summary of the text.*

## Explanation

This standard asks students to establish the essential idea/theme and how it progresses within a literature text, then summarize. With this graphic organizer, students are able to express the central idea/theme in the box at the top and relate how it develops chronologically in the small boxes. Space is provided for a summary as well.

### Central Idea/Theme

| | | |
|---|---|---|
| **Detail 1** | **Detail 2** | **Detail 3** |
| **Detail 4** | **Detail 5** | **Detail 6** |

## Summary:

_____

_____

_____

_____

_____

_____

_____

## CCSS.ELA-Literacy.RL.7.3

Analyze how particular elements of a story or drama interact (e.g., how setting shapes the characters or plot).*

## Explanation

This standard asks students to determine the relationship among a story's setting, characters, and plot. With this graphic organizer, students are able to use the intersecting segments of the circles to document how the story elements interact with each other.

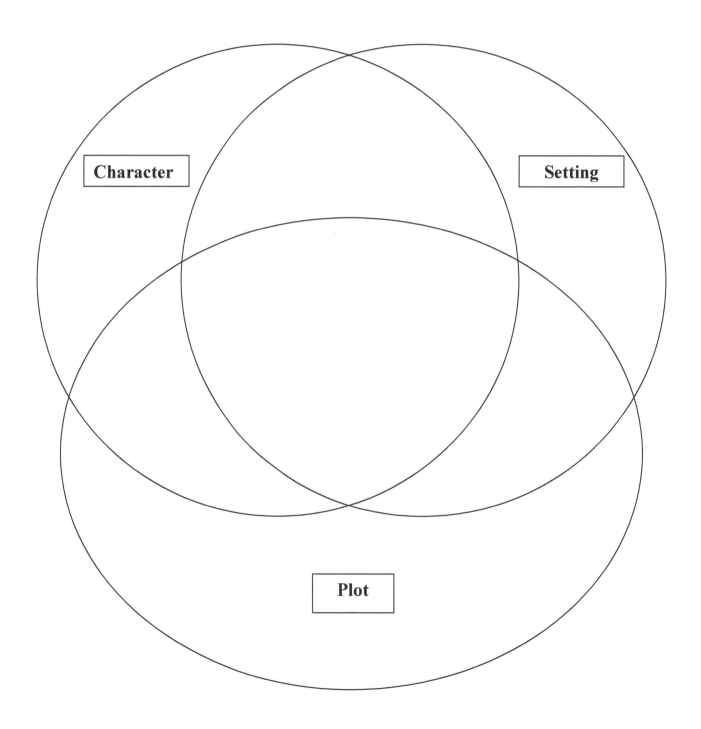

# CCSS.ELA-Literacy.RL.7.4

Determine the meaning of words and phrases as they are used in a text, including figurative and connotative meanings; analyze the impact of rhymes and other repetitions of sounds (e.g., alliteration) on a specific verse or stanza of a poem or story/drama section of a story or drama.*

## Explanation

This standard asks students to establish different meanings for words and phrases in a literature text and determine the relation of rhymes and other repetitions to a particular verse, stanza, or section. With this graphic organizer, students are able to use the left table to write a word or phrase in the first column and describe its various definitions in the second column. Students are able to use the right table to write a rhyme or sound repetition in the first column and analyze its impact on verse, stanza, or section in the second column.

| Word/ Phrase | Definition |
|---|---|
| | Figurative- |
| | Connotative- |

| Literary Device | Impact Analysis |
|---|---|
| Rhymes- | Verse- |
| | Stanza- |
| Sound Repetitions- | |
| | Story/Drama Section- |

# CCSS.ELA-Literacy.RL.7.5

Analyze how a drama's or poem's form or structure (e.g., soliloquy, sonnet) contributes to its meaning.*

## Explanation

This standard asks students to determine the way a literature text's form/structure adds to its meaning. With this graphic organizer, students are able to write the particular type of the literature text in the left column, relate its form/structure in the middle column, and analyze the form's/structure's meaning contribution in the right column.

| Drama/ Poem | Type of Form/ Structure (Choose One: **Drama**-Setup, Conflict, or Resolution. **Poem**-Sililoquy, Sonnet) | Meaning Contribution |
|---|---|---|
| | | |
| | | |

# CCSS.ELA-Literacy.RL.7.6

Analyze how an author develops and contrasts the points of view of different characters or narrators in a text.*

## Explanation

This standard asks students to describe the way an author builds and differentiates various characters' or the narrator's points of view in a literature text. With this graphic organizer, students are able to write the character's or narrator's point of view in the left column, relate how it develops through specific story episodes in the middle column, and explain how that character's/narrator's point of view contrasts others in the story in the right column.

| Character's/ Narrator's Point of View | Development | Contrast to Other Characters/ Narrators |
|---|---|---|
|  | Episode-<br><br><br>Episode-<br><br><br>Episode- |  |

## CCSS.ELA-Literacy.RL.7.7

Compare and contrast a written story, drama, or poem to its audio, filmed, staged, or multimedia version, analyzing the effects of techniques unique to each medium (e.g., lighting, sound, color, or camera focus and angles in a film).*

## Explanation

This standard asks students to note the technique similarities and differences between reading a literature text and viewing or hearing it. With this graphic organizer, students are able to write the name of the work at the top and identify the particular technique in the boxes on the left/right. Then, based on the technique, differences are identified in the non-intersecting parts of the circles, and similarities are identified in the intersection of the two circles.

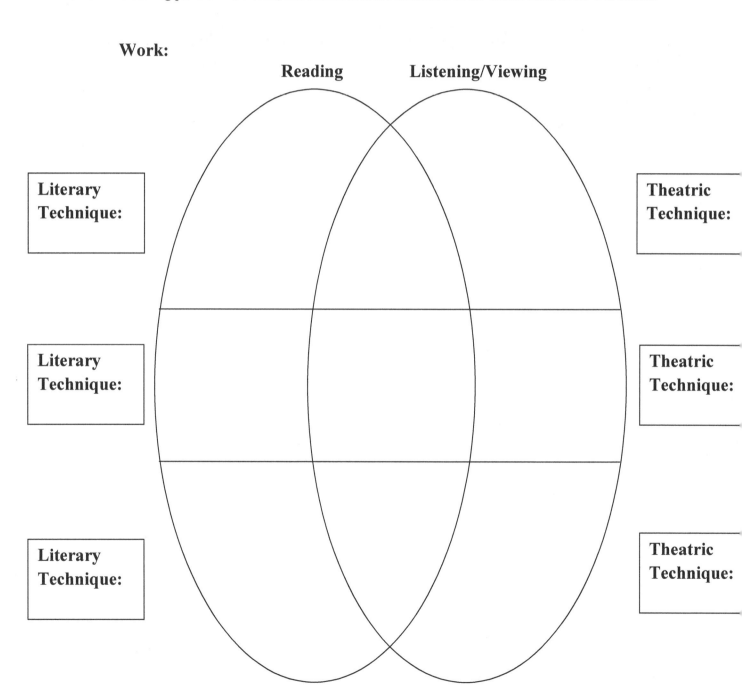

## CCSS.ELA-Literacy.RL.7.9

Compare and contrast a fictional portrayal of a time, place, or character and a historical account of the same period as a means of understanding how authors of fiction use or alter history.*

## Explanation

This standard asks students to note the similarities and differences of reading a fictional text and historical text from the same era and explain how fiction affects history. With this graphic organizer, students are able to write the time, place, or character at the top, identify differences in the non-intersecting parts of the circles, identify similarities in the intersection of the two circles, and explain how fiction alters/uses history in the box on the left.

**Time/Place/Character:**

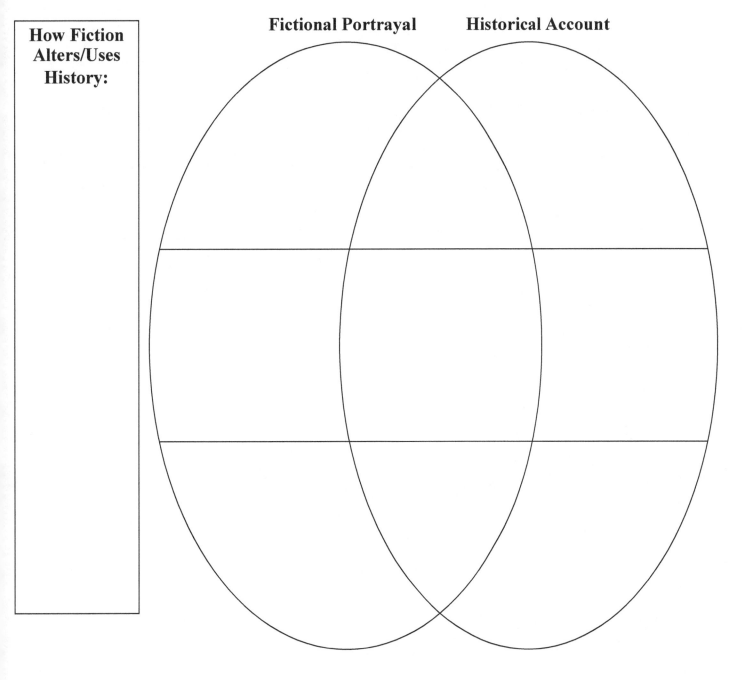

How Fiction Alters/Uses History:

Fictional Portrayal          Historical Account

## <u>CCSS.ELA-Literacy.RL.7.10</u>

By the end of the year, read and comprehend literature, including stories, dramas, and poems, in the grades 6–8 text complexity band proficiently, with scaffolding as needed at the high end of the range.*

## **<u>Explanation</u>**

This standard asks students to read literature texts that are grade-level appropriate. No table or graphic organizer is applicable.

# CHAPTER 8
# 7th Grade Writing

## CCSS.ELA-Literacy.W.7.1

Write arguments to support claims with clear reasons and relevant evidence.*

## CCSS.ELA-Literacy.W.7.1.a

Introduce claim(s), acknowledge alternate or opposing claims, and organize the reasons and evidence logically.*

## CCSS.ELA-Literacy.W.7.1.b

Support claim(s) with logical reasoning and relevant evidence, using accurate, credible sources and demonstrating an understanding of the topic or text.*

## Explanation

This group of standards asks students to write to persuade through the use of claims, reasons, and evidence, while recognizing a counter claim. With this graphic organizer, students are able to brainstorm a claim/alternate claim in the top boxes and reasons, evidence, and sources in the bottom box.

| Claim | Alternate Claim |
|-------|-----------------|
|       |                 |

| Support | Support | Support |
|---------|---------|---------|
| Reason 1- | Reason 2- | Reason 3- |
| Evidence 1- | Evidence 2- | Evidence 3- |
| Source- | Source- | Source- |
| Is it credible?- | Is it credible?- | Is it credible?- |

## CCSS.ELA-Literacy.W.7.1

Write arguments to support claims with clear reasons and relevant evidence.*

## CCSS.ELA-Literacy.W.7.1.c

Use words, phrases, and clauses to create cohesion and clarify the relationships among claim(s), reasons, and evidence.*

## Explanation

This standard asks students to use particular language to associate claim, reasons, and evidence within persuasive writing. With this graphic organizer, students are able to use the top table to write a claim in the left column, write reasons in the middle column, and brainstorm words, phrases, and/or clauses that create cohesion and clarify the relationship among them in the right column. Students are able to use the bottom table to write reasons in the left column, write evidence in the middle column, and brainstorm words, phrases, and/or clauses that create cohesion and clarify the relationship among them in the right column.

| Claim | Reasons | Words/Phrases/Clauses That Clarify |
|---|---|---|
| | 1 | |
| | 2 | |
| | 3 | |

| Reasons | Evidence | Words/Phrases/Clauses That Clarify |
|---|---|---|
| 1 | 1 | |
| 2 | 2 | |
| 3 | 3 | |

## CCSS.ELA-Literacy.W.7.1

Write arguments to support claims with clear reasons and relevant evidence.*

## CCSS.ELA-Literacy.W.7.1.d

Establish and maintain a formal style.*

## Explanation

This standard asks students to have a formal writing style within persuasive writing. Because this standard leaves room for a teacher's interpretation, this example guide allows for modeling and guided practice so that students understand the difference between formal and informal writing styles.

## Informal Writing Style:

_____

_____

_____

_____

_____

_____

_____

## Formal Writing Style:

_____

_____

_____

_____

_____

_____

_____

## CCSS.ELA-Literacy.W.7.1

Write arguments to support claims with clear reasons and relevant evidence.*

## CCSS.ELA-Literacy.W.7.1.e

Provide a concluding statement or section that follows from and supports the argument presented.*

## Explanation

This standard asks students to write a conclusion for persuasive writing. With this graphic organizer, students are able to write claim, reasons, and/or evidence in the top three boxes and, based on that, brainstorm a logical conclusion in the bottom box.

| Claim/Reason/ Evidence 1 | Claim/Reason/ Evidence 2 | Claim/Reason/ Evidence 3 |
|---|---|---|
| | | |

**Conclusion**

## CCSS.ELA-Literacy.W.7.2

Write informative/explanatory texts to examine a topic and convey ideas, concepts, and information through the selection, organization, and analysis of relevant content.*

## CCSS.ELA-Literacy.W.7.2.a

Introduce a topic clearly, previewing what is to follow; organize ideas, concepts, and information, using strategies such as definition, classification, comparison/contrast, and cause/effect; include formatting (e.g., headings), graphics (e.g., charts, tables), and multimedia when useful to aiding comprehension.*

## Explanation

This standard asks students to utilize the elements of introduction, organization, formatting, and graphics/multimedia for informative/explanatory writing. With this graphic organizer, students are able to write the topic at the top and brainstorm an introduction in the first table, an organization strategy in the second table, formatting in the third table, and graphics/multimedia in the fourth table.

**Topic:**

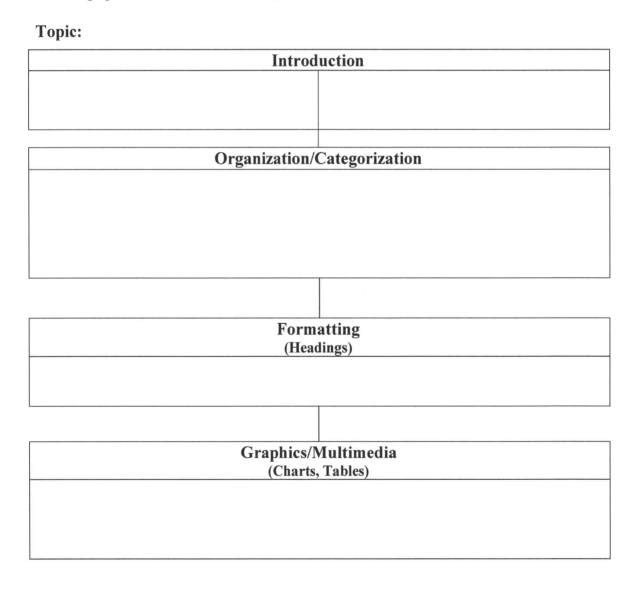

## CCSS.ELA-Literacy.W.7.2

Write informative/explanatory texts to examine a topic and convey ideas, concepts, and information through the selection, organization, and analysis of relevant content.*

## CCSS.ELA-Literacy.W.7.2.b

Develop the topic with relevant facts, definitions, concrete details, quotations, or other information and examples.*

## Explanation

This standard asks students to have the micro elements of facts, definitions, details, quotations, and examples within informative/explanatory writing. With this graphic organizer, students are able to write the topic at the top and brainstorm these elements inside.

**Topic:**

| Development |
|---|
| Facts- |
| Definitions- |
| Concrete Details- |
| Quotations- |
| Other Information/Examples- |

## CCSS.ELA-Literacy.W.7.2

Write informative/explanatory texts to examine a topic and convey ideas, concepts, and information through the selection, organization, and analysis of relevant content.*

## CCSS.ELA-Literacy.W.7.2.c

Use appropriate transitions to create cohesion and clarify the relationships among ideas and concepts.*

## Explanation

This standard asks students to use particular language to associate ideas and concepts within informative/explanatory writing. With this graphic organizer, students are able to write their ideas and concepts in the left table and brainstorm transitions that create cohesion and clarify how they relate in the right boxes.

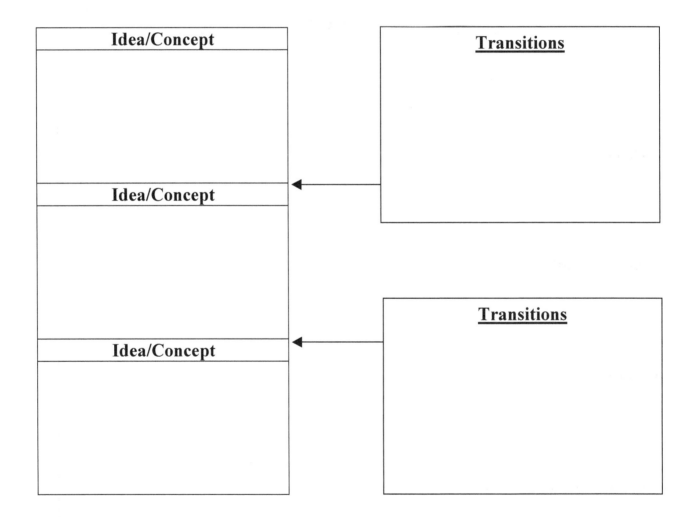

## <u>CCSS.ELA-Literacy.W.7.2</u>

Write informative/explanatory texts to examine a topic and convey ideas, concepts, and information through the selection, organization, and analysis of relevant content.*

## <u>CCSS.ELA-Literacy.W.7.2.d</u>

Use precise language and domain-specific vocabulary to inform about or explain the topic.*

## <u>Explanation</u>

This standard asks students to utilize certain subject matter words within informative/explanatory writing. With this graphic organizer, students are able to write the topic at the top and brainstorm precise domain-specific vocabulary that relates to the topic inside.

### Topic:

| Precise/Domain-Specific Vocabulary |
|:---:|
|  |

# CCSS.ELA-Literacy.W.7.2

Write informative/explanatory texts to examine a topic and convey ideas, concepts, and information through the selection, organization, and analysis of relevant content.*

# CCSS.ELA-Literacy.W.7.2.e

Establish and maintain a formal style.*

# Explanation

This standard asks students to have a formal writing style within informative/explanatory writing. Because this standard leaves room for a teacher's interpretation, this example guide allows for modeling and guided practice so that students understand the difference between formal and informal writing styles.

## Informal Writing Style:

_____

_____

_____

_____

_____

_____

_____

## Formal Writing Style:

_____

_____

_____

_____

_____

_____

_____

_____

## CCSS.ELA-Literacy.W.7.2

Write informative/explanatory texts to examine a topic and convey ideas, concepts, and information through the selection, organization, and analysis of relevant content.*

## CCSS.ELA-Literacy.W.7.2.f

Provide a concluding statement or section that follows from and supports the information or explanation presented.*

## Explanation

This standard asks students to write a conclusion for informative/explanatory writing. With this graphic organizer, students are able to write concepts or ideas presented in the top three boxes and, based on that, brainstorm a logical conclusion in the bottom box.

| Concept/Idea 1 | Concept/Idea 2 | Concept/Idea 3 |
|---|---|---|
|  |  |  |

**Conclusion**

# CCSS.ELA-Literacy.W.7.3

Write narratives to develop real or imagined experiences or events using effective technique, relevant descriptive details, and well-structured event sequences.*

# CCSS.ELA-Literacy.W.7.3.a

Engage and orient the reader by establishing a context and point of view and introducing a narrator and/or characters; organize an event sequence that unfolds naturally and logically.*

# CCSS.ELA-Literacy.W.7.3.b

Use narrative techniques, such as dialogue, pacing, and description, to develop experiences, events, and/or characters.*

# CCSS.ELA-Literacy.W.7.3.d

Use precise words and phrases, relevant descriptive details, and sensory language to capture the action and convey experiences and events.*

# Explanation

This group of standards asks students to have the macro elements of context, point of view, characters, and event sequence and micro elements of dialogue, pacing, description, precise language, relevant descriptive details, and sensory language that develop experiences, events, and/or characters in narrative writing. With this graphic organizer, students are able to brainstorm these elements, making sure they relate to each other.

## Establish

| |
|---|
| **Context:** |
| **Characters/Narrator:** |
| **Point of View:** |

## Event Sequence

| Event 1 | **Narrative Technique (Choose):** Dialogue, Pacing, or Description | **To Develop (Choose):** |
|---|---|---|
| | precise words and phrases, relevant descriptive details, and sensory language: | Events, Experiences, or Characters |

*Continued on next page

| Event 2 | **Narrative Technique (Choose):** <br> Dialogue, Pacing, or Description | **To Develop (Choose):** |
|---|---|---|
| | precise words and phrases, relevant descriptive details, and sensory language: | Events, Experiences, or Characters |

| Event 3 | **Narrative Technique (Choose):** <br> Dialogue, Pacing, or Description | **To Develop (Choose):** |
|---|---|---|
| | precise words and phrases, relevant descriptive details, and sensory language: | Events, Experiences, or Characters |

| Event 4 | **Narrative Technique (Choose):** <br> Dialogue, Pacing, or Description | **To Develop (Choose):** |
|---|---|---|
| | precise words and phrases, relevant descriptive details, and sensory language: | Events, Experiences, or Characters |

| Event 5 | **Narrative Technique (Choose):** <br> Dialogue, Pacing, or Description | **To Develop (Choose):** |
|---|---|---|
| | precise words and phrases, relevant descriptive details, and sensory language: | Events, Experiences, or Characters |

## CCSS.ELA-Literacy.W.7.3

Write narratives to develop real or imagined experiences or events using effective technique, relevant descriptive details, and well-structured event sequences.*

## CCSS.ELA-Literacy.W.7.3.c

Use a variety of transition words, phrases, and clauses to convey sequence and signal shifts from one time frame or setting to another.*

## Explanation

This standard asks students to use particular language to express time progression within narrative writing. With this graphic organizer, students are able to write events in the left table and brainstorm words, phrases, and clauses that convey sequence and signal shifts from one time frame or setting to another in the right boxes.

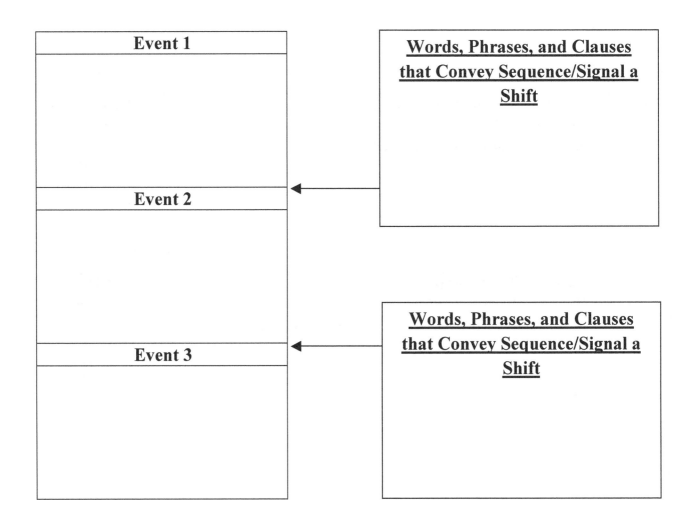

## CCSS.ELA-Literacy.W.7.3

Write narratives to develop real or imagined experiences or events using effective technique, relevant descriptive details, and well-structured event sequences.*

## CCSS.ELA-Literacy.W.7.3.e

Provide a conclusion that follows from and reflects on the narrated experiences or events.*

## Explanation

This standard asks students to write a conclusion for narrative writing. With this graphic organizer, students are able to write experiences or events of the narrative in the top three boxes and, based on that, brainstorm a logical conclusion in the bottom box.

| Event/Experience 1 | Event/Experience 2 | Event/Experience 3 |
|---|---|---|
|  |  |  |

**Conclusion**

## CCSS.ELA-Literacy.W.7.4

Produce clear and coherent writing in which the development, organization, and style are appropriate to task, purpose, and audience. (Grade-specific expectations for writing types are defined in standards 1–3 above.)*

## Explanation

This standard asks students to have clear/coherent writing for persuasive, informative/explanatory, and narrative texts. Because this standard leaves room for a teacher's interpretation, this example guide allows for modeling and guided practice so that students understand the difference between unclear/incoherent and clear/coherent writing styles.

## Unclear/Incoherent Writing Style:

_____

_____

_____

_____

_____

_____

_____

## Clear/Coherent Writing Style:

_____

_____

_____

_____

_____

_____

_____

## CCSS.ELA-Literacy.W.7.5

With some guidance and support from peers and adults, develop and strengthen writing as needed by planning, revising, editing, rewriting, or trying a new approach, focusing on how well purpose and audience have been addressed. (Editing for conventions should demonstrate command of Language standards 1–3 up to and including grade 7 here.)*

## Explanation

This standard asks students to use the writing process for persuasive, informative/explanatory, and narrative texts. No table or graphic organizer is applicable.

## CCSS.ELA-Literacy.W.7.6

Use technology, including the Internet, to produce and publish writing and link to and cite sources as well as to interact and collaborate with others, including linking to and citing sources.*

## Explanation

This standard asks students to use technology for persuasive, informative/explanatory, and narrative texts. No table or graphic organizer is applicable.

# CCSS.ELA-Literacy.W.7.7

Conduct short research projects to answer a question, drawing on several sources and generating additional related, focused questions for further research and investigation.*

# Explanation

This standard asks students to find information from various sources for research writing and create questions connected to the research question. With this graphic organizer, students are able to write their research question at the top, identify information from various sources in the big boxes, make sure it is related to their research question at the top, and identify additional related, focused questions in the small boxes.

**Research Question-**

**Source #1/Findings**

**Source #2/Findings**

**Additional Questions**

**Source #3/Findings**

**Additional Questions**

## CCSS.ELA-Literacy.W.7.8

Gather relevant information from multiple print and digital sources, using search terms effectively; assess the credibility and accuracy of each source; and quote or paraphrase the data and conclusions of others while avoiding plagiarism and following a standard format for citation.*

## Explanation

This standard asks students to find pertinent information, utilize searches, evaluate the value of the information, quote/paraphrase the information without plagiarism, and cite sources. With this graphic organizer, students are able to use the top table to write the research question/topic at the top and brainstorm related search terms inside. Students are able to use the bottom table to quote and/or paraphrase findings in the second column, cite sources in the third column, and assess credibility of those sources in the fourth column.

### Research Question/Topic-

| Search Terms: |
| --- |
| |

| | Findings | Sources in Bibliographical Form | Source Credibility |
| --- | --- | --- | --- |
| **Quote** | | | |
| **Paraphrase** | | | |

## CCSS.ELA-Literacy.W.7.9

Draw evidence from literary or informational texts to support analysis, reflection, and research.*

## CCSS.ELA-Literacy.W.7.9.a

Apply *grade 7 Reading standards* to literature (e.g., "Compare and contrast a fictional portrayal of a time, place, or character and a historical account of the same period as a means of understanding how authors of fiction use or alter history").*

## CCSS.ELA-Literacy.W.7.9.b

Apply *grade 7 Reading standards* to literary nonfiction (e.g. "Trace and evaluate the argument and specific claims in a text, assessing whether the reasoning is sound and the evidence is relevant and sufficient to support the claims").*

## Explanation

This group of standards asks students to write for the purpose of expressing the reading standards. With the first example guide, students are able to link a literature reading standard at the top to related analysis, reflection, and research below it. With the second example guide, students are able to link a literary nonfiction reading standard at the top to related analysis, reflection, and research below it.

**Literature Standard:**_____

**Analysis/Reflection/Research:**

_____

_____

_____

_____

_____

**Nonfiction Standard:**_____

**Analysis/Reflection/Research:**

_____

_____

_____

_____

_____

## CCSS.ELA-Literacy.W.7.10

Write routinely over extended time frames (time for research, reflection, and revision) and shorter time frames (a single sitting or a day or two) for a range of discipline-specific tasks, purposes, and audiences.*

## Explanation

This standard asks students to write short and long pieces of writing. No table or graphic organizer is applicable.

# CHAPTER 9

# 7th Grade Speaking/Listening

## CCSS.ELA-Literacy.SL.7.1

Engage effectively in a range of collaborative discussions (one-on-one, in groups, and teacher-led) with diverse partners on grade 7 topics, texts, and issues, building on others' ideas and expressing their own clearly.*

## CCSS.ELA-Literacy.SL.7.1.a

Come to discussions prepared, having read or researched material under study; explicitly draw on that preparation by referring to evidence on the topic, text, or issue to probe and reflect on ideas under discussion.*

## Explanation

This standard asks students to be ready with topical evidence for class discussions. With this graphic organizer, students are able to write the topic/text/issue at the top and prepare using an outline, a graphic organizer, or both.

### Topic/Text/Issue of Discussion:

| Evidence From Reading/Studying: | Evidence From Reading/Studying: |
|---|---|
| I.<br>A.<br>B.<br>C.<br><br>II.<br>A.<br>B.<br>C.<br><br>III.<br>A.<br>B.<br>C.<br><br>IV.<br>A.<br>B.<br>C.<br><br>V.<br>A.<br>B.<br>C. | |

## CCSS.ELA-Literacy.SL.7.1

Engage effectively in a range of collaborative discussions (one-on-one, in groups, and teacher-led) with diverse partners on grade 7 topics, texts, and issues, building on others' ideas and expressing their own clearly.*

## CCSS.ELA-Literacy.SL.7.1.b

Follow rules for collegial discussions, track progress toward specific goals and deadlines, and define individual roles as needed.*

## Explanation

This standard asks students to participate in setting and tracking class discussion norms. With this graphic organizer, students are able to write the topic/issue at the top, propose rules, goals, deadlines, and roles in the middle column, and track their progress in the right column.

### Topic/Issue of Discussion:

| Rules | | Progress Check/Reflection: |
|---|---|---|
| Goals | | Progress Check/Reflection: |
| Deadlines | | Progress Check/Reflection: |
| Individual Roles | | Progress Check/Reflection: |

## CCSS.ELA-Literacy.SL.7.1

Engage effectively in a range of collaborative discussions (one-on-one, in groups, and teacher-led) with diverse partners on grade 7 topics, texts, and issues, building on others' ideas and expressing their own clearly.*

## CCSS.ELA-Literacy.SL.7.1.c

Pose questions that elicit elaboration and respond to others' questions and comments with relevant observations and ideas that bring the discussion back on topic as needed.*

## Explanation

This standard asks students to participate in class discussion with questions that require explanation and comments that represent observations and ideas. With this graphic organizer, students are able to write the topic/issue at the top, capture others' comments in the left column, write their related questions that elicit elaboration in the middle column, and document their responses in the right column.

**Topic/Issue of Discussion:**

| Others' Comments | My Questions that Elicit Elaboration | My Responses (Using Observations/Ideas) |
|---|---|---|
|  |  |  |
|  |  |  |
|  |  |  |

## CCSS.ELA-Literacy.SL.7.1

Engage effectively in a range of collaborative discussions (one-on-one, in groups, and teacher-led) with diverse partners on grade 7 topics, texts, and issues, building on others' ideas and expressing their own clearly.*

## CCSS.ELA-Literacy.SL.7.1.d

Acknowledge new information expressed by others and, when warranted, modify their own views.*

## Explanation

This standard asks students to recognize new knowledge communicated in class discussions and possibly change their perspective based on that. With this graphic organizer, students are able to write the topic/issue under discussion and their view above, record information expressed by others in the left column, and modify their view in the right column.

## Topic/Issue of Discussion:

**Your View:**

_____

_____

_____

| **Information Expressed by Others** | **Modification of Your View** |
|---|---|
| | |
| | |
| | |

## CCSS.ELA-Literacy.SL.7.2

Analyze the main ideas and supporting details presented in diverse media and formats (e.g., visually, quantitatively, orally) and explain how the ideas clarify a topic, text, or issue under study.*

## Explanation

This standard asks students to examine the main ideas and details of various types of given material and describe how it has provided clarity. With this graphic organizer, students are able to write the topic/text/issue at the top, analyze the main ideas and details presented in diverse media and formats in the left column, and explain how the ideas clarify the topic, text, or issue under study in the right column.

### Topic/Text/Issue Under Study:

| Analysis | How Topic, Text, or Issue Has Been Clarified |
|---|---|
| **Visual Information:**<br>I.<br>A.<br>B.<br>C.<br>II.<br>A.<br>B.<br>C.<br>III.<br>A.<br>B.<br>C. | |
| **Quantitative Information:**<br>I.<br>A.<br>B.<br>C.<br>II.<br>A.<br>B.<br>C.<br>III.<br>A.<br>B.<br>C. | |
| **Oral Information:**<br>I.<br>A.<br>B.<br>C.<br>II.<br>A.<br>B.<br>C.<br>III.<br>A.<br>B.<br>C. | |

# CCSS.ELA-Literacy.SL.7.3

Delineate a speaker's argument and specific claims, evaluating the soundness of the reasoning and the relevance and sufficiency of the evidence.*

## Explanation

This standard asks students to outline and assess a speaker's argument or claim in terms of reasons and evidence. With this graphic organizer, students are able to write the speaker's argument or claim in the top box, delineate reasons and evidence for that claim in the left column, and evaluate reasons and evidence in the right column.

### Argument/Claim

| Delineation | Evaluation |
|---|---|
| Reasons- | Soundness of Reasons- |
| Evidence- | Relevancy/Sufficiency of Evidence- |

# CCSS.ELA-Literacy.SL.7.4

Present claims and findings, emphasizing salient points in a focused, coherent manner with pertinent descriptions, facts, details, and examples; use appropriate eye contact, adequate volume, and clear pronunciation.*

## Explanation

This standard asks students to be ready for class speeches with significant, logical topic information, explanations, and evidence. With this graphic organizer, students are able to write the finding/claim at the top and express these elements using an outline, a graphic organizer, or both.

### Finding/Claim:

| Descriptions, Facts, Details, and Examples: | Descriptions, Facts, Details, and Examples: |
|---|---|
| I. <br> A. <br> B. <br> C. <br><br> II. <br> A. <br> B. <br> C. <br><br> III. <br> A. <br> B. <br> C. <br><br> IV. <br> A. <br> B. <br> C. <br><br> V. <br> A. <br> B. <br> C. | |

## <u>CCSS.ELA-Literacy.SL.7.5</u>

Include multimedia components and visual displays in presentations to clarify claims and findings and emphasize salient points.*

## <u>Explanation</u>

This standard asks students to be ready for class speeches using interactive media elements and visuals in a strategic manner. With this graphic organizer, students are able to brainstorm what they intend to present in the left column, relate what multimedia/visuals could be utilized in the middle column, and explain how the multimedia/visuals clarify claims and findings and emphasize salient points in the right column.

| Presentation Information (Main Ideas) | Possible Multimedia/Visual Components | How the Multimedia/Visual Components Clarify/Emphasize |
|---|---|---|
| | | |
| | | |
| | | |

## <u>CCSS.ELA-Literacy.SL.7.6</u>

Adapt speech to a variety of contexts and tasks, demonstrating command of formal English when indicated or appropriate. (See grade 7 Language standards 1 and 3 here for specific expectations.)*

## <u>Explanation</u>

This standard asks students to speak within a range of grade-level situations. No table or graphic organizer is applicable.

# CHAPTER 10

# 7th Grade Language

## CCSS.ELA-Literacy.L.7.1

Demonstrate command of the conventions of standard English grammar and usage when writing or speaking.*

## CCSS.ELA-Literacy.L.7.1.a

Explain the function of phrases and clauses in general and their function in specific sentences.*

## Explanation

This standard asks students to clarify the purpose of phrases and clauses. With this graphic organizer, students are able to write a particular phrase or clause in the left column, use it in a sentence in the middle column, and explain its function in the right column.

| Phrase/ Clause | Sentence Example | Explanation |
|---|---|---|
| | | **General Function-** <br><br> **Specific Function in Example-** |
| | | **General Function-** <br><br> **Specific Function in Example-** |
| | | **General Function-** <br><br> **Specific Function in Example-** |

## CCSS.ELA-Literacy.L.7.1

Demonstrate command of the conventions of standard English grammar and usage when writing or speaking.*

## CCSS.ELA-Literacy.L.7.1.b

Choose among simple, compound, complex, and compound-complex sentences to signal differing relationships among ideas.*

## Explanation

This standard asks students to utilize a particular sentence that indicates how various concepts connect. With this graphic organizer and example guide, students are able to brainstorm ideas in the boxes at the top, write the relationship of stated ideas above each example guide, use the example guide to consciously choose the type of sentence that best signals the differing relationships among ideas, and write the chosen sentence that signals differing relationships among ideas.

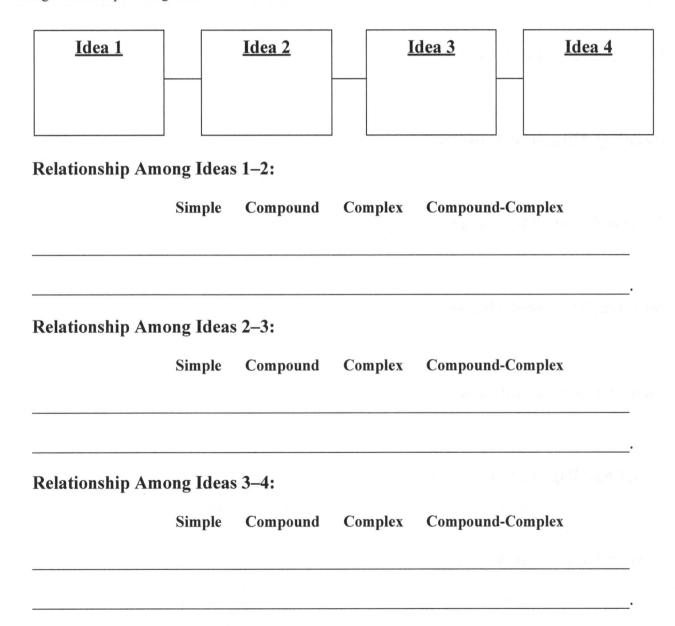

| Idea 1 | Idea 2 | Idea 3 | Idea 4 |

**Relationship Among Ideas 1–2:**

        **Simple**    **Compound**    **Complex**    **Compound-Complex**

_____

_____ .

**Relationship Among Ideas 2–3:**

        **Simple**    **Compound**    **Complex**    **Compound-Complex**

_____

_____ .

**Relationship Among Ideas 3–4:**

        **Simple**    **Compound**    **Complex**    **Compound-Complex**

_____

_____ .

## CCSS.ELA-Literacy.L.7.1

Demonstrate command of the conventions of standard English grammar and usage when writing or speaking.*

## CCSS.ELA-Literacy.L.7.1.c

Place phrases and clauses within a sentence, recognizing and correcting misplaced and dangling modifiers.*

## Explanation

This standard asks students to use phrases and clauses in sentences, notice mistakes in their use, and rectify misplaced and dangling modifiers. With this example guide, students are given space to discern the difference between misplaced/dangling and correct clause/phrase use.

## Dangling/Misplaced Modifier:

_____

## Correct Clause/Phrase Use:

_____

## Dangling/Misplaced Modifier:

_____

## Correct Clause/Phrase Use:

_____

## Dangling/Misplaced Modifier:

_____

## Correct Clause/Phrase Use:

_____

## Dangling/Misplaced Modifier:

_____

## Correct Clause/Phrase Use:

_____

## CCSS.ELA-Literacy.L.7.2

Demonstrate command of the conventions of standard English capitalization, punctuation, and spelling when writing.*

## CCSS.ELA-Literacy.L.7.2.a

Use a comma to separate coordinate adjectives (e.g., *It was a fascinating, enjoyable movie* but not *He wore an old[,] green shirt*).*

## Explanation

This standard asks students to utilize commas to separate a set of adjectives. With this example guide, students are given space to brainstorm adjectives to be used and write sentences using those adjectives.

**Adjectives to be used:**

_____

_____

_____

_____

**Adjectives to be used:**

_____

_____

_____

_____

**Adjectives to be used:**

_____

_____

_____

_____

**Adjectives to be used:**

_____

_____

_____

_____

## CCSS.ELA-Literacy.L.7.2

Demonstrate command of the conventions of standard English capitalization, punctuation, and spelling when writing.*

## CCSS.ELA-Literacy.L.7.2.b

Spell correctly.*

## Explanation

This standard asks students to spell words precisely. No table or graphic organizer is applicable.

## CCSS.ELA-Literacy.L.7.3

Use knowledge of language and its conventions when writing, speaking, reading, or listening.*

## CCSS.ELA-Literacy.L.7.3.a

Choose language that expresses ideas precisely and concisely, recognizing and eliminating wordiness and redundancy.*

## Explanation

This standard asks students to communicate in an accurate and succinct manner. Because this standard leaves room for a teacher's interpretation, this example guide allows for modeling and guided practice so that students understand the difference between inaccurate/wordy communication and precise/concise communication.

## Inaccurate/Wordy Writing:

_____

_____

_____

_____

_____

_____

_____

_____

## Precise/Concise Writing:

_____

_____

_____

_____

_____

_____

_____

_____

# CCSS.ELA-Literacy.L.7.4

Determine or clarify the meaning of unknown and multiple-meaning words and phrases based on *grade 7 reading and content*, choosing flexibly from a range of strategies.*

# CCSS.ELA-Literacy.L.7.4.a

Use context (e.g., the overall meaning of a sentence or paragraph; a word's position or function in a sentence) as a clue to the meaning of a word or phrase.*

# Explanation

This standard asks students to utilize context for word definition clues. With this graphic organizer, students are able to write the unknown word or phrase in the left column, relate given clues to its meaning in the middle column, and make an educated guess about its definition in the right column.

| Unknown Word/Phrase | Possible Clue Words/ Overall Meaning/ Position or Function | Possible Meaning of Unknown Word/Phrase |
|---|---|---|
|  |  |  |
|  |  |  |
|  |  |  |
|  |  |  |
|  |  |  |
|  |  |  |
|  |  |  |

## CCSS.ELA-Literacy.L.7.4

Determine or clarify the meaning of unknown and multiple-meaning words and phrases based on *grade 7 reading and content*, choosing flexibly from a range of strategies.*

## CCSS.ELA-Literacy.L.7.4.b

Use common, grade-appropriate Greek or Latin affixes and roots as clues to the meaning of a word (e.g., *belligerent, bellicose, rebel*).*

## Explanation

This standard asks students to utilize affixes/roots as word definition clues. With this graphic organizer, students are able to use the first table to identify affixes/roots in the first and third columns and write definitions next to each. Students are able to use the second table to write an unknown word in the left column, pick out its affix/root in the middle column, and based on the affix/root definition from the first table, make an educated guess about the unknown word's definition in the right column.

| 7th Grade Affix/Root | Definition | 7th Grade Affix/Root | Definition |
|---|---|---|---|
| | | | |
| | | | |
| | | | |
| | | | |
| | | | |
| | | | |
| | | | |
| | | | |
| | | | |
| | | | |
| | | | |

| Unknown Word | Affix/Root | Possible Definition of Unknown Word |
|---|---|---|
| | | |
| | | |
| | | |
| | | |

## CCSS.ELA-Literacy.L.7.4

Determine or clarify the meaning of unknown and multiple-meaning words and phrases based on *grade 7 reading and content*, choosing flexibly from a range of strategies.*

## CCSS.ELA-Literacy.L.7.4.c

Consult general and specialized reference materials (e.g., dictionaries, glossaries, thesauruses), both print and digital, to find the pronunciation of a word or determine or clarify its precise meaning or its part of speech.*

## Explanation

This standard asks students to utilize reference resources for unknown words. With this graphic organizer, students are able to write the unknown word in the left column and relate its definition, part of speech, and pronunciation from a reference material in the right column.

| Unknown Word | Reference Material-Definition/Part of Speech/Pronunciation |
|---|---|
|  |  |
|  |  |
|  |  |
|  |  |
|  |  |
|  |  |
|  |  |
|  |  |
|  |  |
|  |  |
|  |  |
|  |  |
|  |  |

## CCSS.ELA-Literacy.L.7.4

Determine or clarify the meaning of unknown and multiple-meaning words and phrases based on *grade 7 reading and content*, choosing flexibly from a range of strategies.*

## CCSS.ELA-Literacy.L.7.4.d

Verify the preliminary determination of the meaning of a word or phrase (e.g., by checking the inferred meaning in context or in a dictionary).*

## Explanation

This standard asks students to utilize context and dictionaries for word definition confirmation. With this graphic organizer, students are able to write the unknown word or phrase in the left column, relate its preliminary meaning in the middle column, and verify the definition in the right column.

| Word/Phrase | Preliminary Determination of Meaning | Inferred Meaning in Context/Dictionary |
|---|---|---|
| | | |
| | | |
| | | |
| | | |
| | | |
| | | |
| | | |
| | | |
| | | |
| | | |
| | | |
| | | |
| | | |

## CCSS.ELA-Literacy.L.7.5

Demonstrate understanding of figurative language, word relationships, and nuances in word meanings.*

## CCSS.ELA-Literacy.L.7.5.a

Interpret figures of speech (e.g., literary, biblical, and mythological allusions) in context.*

## Explanation

This standard asks students to explain figures of speech. With this graphic organizer, students are able to write the figure of speech in the top row and interpret it in the bottom row.

| **Figure of Speech** (Literary, Biblical, and Mythological Allusions) | | | |
|---|---|---|---|
| **Interpretation** | | | |

## CCSS.ELA-Literacy.L.7.5

Demonstrate understanding of figurative language, word relationships, and nuances in word meanings.*

## CCSS.ELA-Literacy.L.7.5.b

Use the relationship between particular words (e.g., synonym/antonym, analogy) to better understand each of the words.*

## Explanation

This standard asks students to utilize word relationships as clues to their meaning. With this graphic organizer, students are able to write two associated words in columns one and two based on the relationship stated in the third column and explain the two associated words in the fourth column.

| Word 1 | Word 2 | Relationship<br><br>cause/effect | Explanation<br>1-<br>2- |
|---|---|---|---|
| Word 1 | Word 2 | Relationship<br><br>object/function | Explanation<br>1-<br>2- |
| Word 1 | Word 2 | Relationship<br><br>item/category | Explanation<br>1-<br>2- |
| Word 1 | Word 2 | Relationship<br><br>synonym | Explanation<br>1-<br>2- |
| Word 1 | Word 2 | Relationship<br><br>antonym | Explanation<br>1-<br>2- |
| Word 1 | Word 2 | Relationship<br><br>part/whole | Explanation<br>1-<br>2- |

## CCSS.ELA-Literacy.L.7.5

Demonstrate understanding of figurative language, word relationships, and nuances in word meanings.*

## CCSS.ELA-Literacy.L.7.5.c

Distinguish among the connotations (associations) of words with similar denotations (definitions) (e.g., *refined, respectful, polite, diplomatic, condescending*).*

## Explanation

This standard asks students to notice the differences between the connotations and denotations of a group of words. With this graphic organizer, students are able to write similar words in the top row, relate their similar denotations in the middle row, and determine each word's connotation in the bottom row.

| Similar Words | | | |
|---|---|---|---|
| **Denotation** | | | |
| **Connotation** | | | |
| **Similar Words** | | | |
| **Denotation** | | | |
| **Connotation** | | | |
| **Similar Words** | | | |
| **Denotation** | | | |
| **Connotation** | | | |

## CCSS.ELA-Literacy.L.7.6

Acquire and use accurately grade-appropriate general academic and domain-specific words and phrases; gather vocabulary knowledge when considering a word or phrase important to comprehension or expression.*

## Explanation

This standard asks students to use vocabulary that is grade-level appropriate and collect vocabulary information. For the former, no table or graphic organizer is applicable, and the latter is addressed in CCSS.ELA-Literacy.L.7.4.

# Section 3

## 8th Grade

## Graphic Organizers

# CHAPTER 11

# 8th Grade
# Reading Informational Text

## CCSS.ELA-Literacy.RI.8.1

Cite the textual evidence that most strongly supports an analysis of what the text says explicitly as well as inferences drawn from the text.*

## Explanation

This standard asks students to indicate the most powerful proof of explicit and inferential meaning within an informational text. With this graphic organizer, students are able to analyze for explicit and inferential meaning in the top row, relate various pieces of evidence for those individual meanings in the middle row, and explain the strongest piece of evidence in the bottom row.

| | |
|---|---|
| **Explicit Meaning** | |
| **Textual Evidence** | -<br>-<br>- |
| **Which Evidence is the Strongest? Why?** | |

| | |
|---|---|
| **Inferential Meaning** | |
| **Textual Evidence** | -<br>-<br>- |
| **Which Evidence is the Strongest? Why?** | |

# CCSS.ELA-Literacy.RI.8.2

Determine a central idea of a text and analyze its development over the course of the text, including its relationship to supporting ideas; provide an objective summary of the text.*

## Explanation

This standard asks students to establish the essential idea and examine how it progresses and connects to supporting details within an informational text, then summarize. With this graphic organizer, students are able to express the central idea in the big box at the top and relate how details develop/relate to the central idea in the small boxes. Space is provided for a summary as well.

**Central Idea**

| | | |
|---|---|---|
| **Detail 1** | **Detail 2** | **Detail 3** |
| **Relation to Central Idea** | **Relation to Central Idea** | **Relation to Central Idea** |

**Summary:**

_____

_____

_____

_____

_____

_____

_____

## CCSS.ELA-Literacy.RI.8.3

Analyze how a text makes connections among and distinctions between individuals, ideas, or events (e.g., through comparisons, analogies, or categories).*

## Explanation

This standard asks students to examine how an informational text creates associations and differences between individuals, events, and ideas by using comparisons, analogies, or categories. With this graphic organizer, students are able to use the intersecting segments of the circles to document how individuals, ideas, or events connect among each other and the non-intersecting segments of the circles to document how individuals, ideas, or events are distinct from each other.

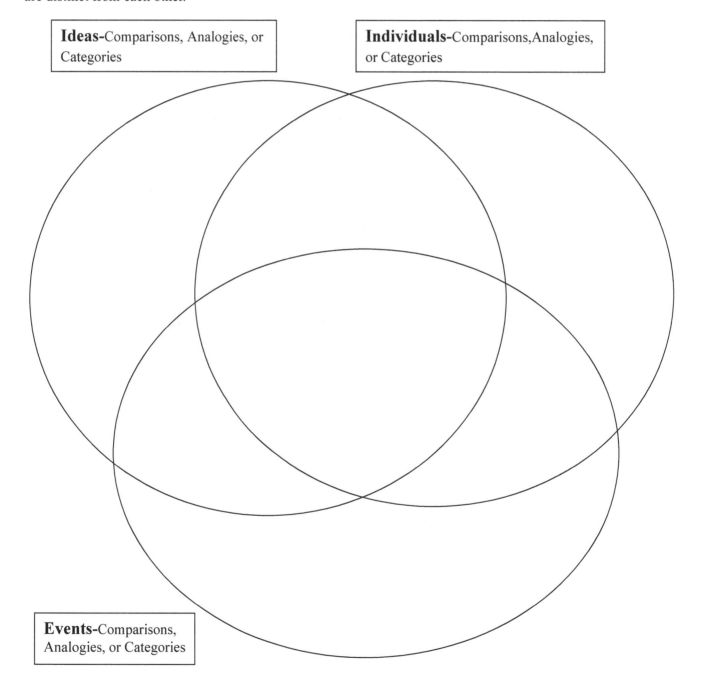

**Ideas**-Comparisons, Analogies, or Categories

**Individuals**-Comparisons, Analogies, or Categories

**Events**-Comparisons, Analogies, or Categories

# CCSS.ELA-Literacy.RI.8.4

Determine the meaning of words and phrases as they are used in a text, including figurative, connotative, and technical meanings; analyze the impact of specific word choices on meaning and tone, including analogies or allusions to other texts.*

## Explanation

This standard asks students to establish different meanings for words and phrases in an informational text and determine the relation of word choice to meaning and tone. With this graphic organizer, students are able to use the left table to write a word or phrase in the first column and describe its various definitions in the second column. Students are able to use the right table to write a specific word choice in the first column and analyze its impact on meaning and tone in the second column.

| Word/ Phrase | Definition |
|---|---|
| | Figurative- <br><br><br> Connotative- <br><br><br> Technical- |

| Specific Word Choice | Impact Analysis |
|---|---|
| Analogies- <br><br><br><br> Allusions to Other Texts- | Meaning- <br><br><br><br> Tone- |

# CCSS.ELA-Literacy.RI.8.5

Analyze in detail the structure of a specific paragraph in a text, including the role of particular sentences in developing and refining a key concept.*

# Explanation

This standard asks students to determine how paragraph structure and specific sentences advance an important idea in an informational text. With this graphic organizer, students are able to write particular sentences that develop a key concept in the left column, relate the role of those particular sentences in developing/refining that key concept in the middle column, and note the paragraph structure in the right column.

| Particular Sentences | Particular Sentences' Development/Refinement Role for a Key Concept | Paragraph Structure (Choose One: Chronological/Sequence, Cause/Effect, Problem/Solution, Compare/Contrast, Description, Directions) |
|---|---|---|
|  |  |  |
|  |  |  |

# CCSS.ELA-Literacy.RI.8.6

Determine an author's point of view or purpose in a text and analyze how the author acknowledges and responds to conflicting evidence or viewpoints.*

## Explanation

This standard asks students to establish an author's point of view or purpose in an informational text and examine how he/she recognizes and counters opposing evidence/viewpoints. With this graphic organizer, students are able to write the author's point of view or purpose in the left column, analyze how he/she acknowledges conflicting evidence/viewpoints in the middle column, and analyze how he/she responds to conflicting evidence/viewpoints in the right column.

| Author's Point of View/Purpose | Author's Acknowledgment of Conflicting Evidence/Viewpoints | Author's Response to Conflicting Evidence/Viewpoints |
|---|---|---|
| | | |

## CCSS.ELA-Literacy.RI.8.7

Evaluate the advantages and disadvantages of using different mediums (e.g., print or digital text, video, multimedia) to present a particular topic or idea.*

## Explanation

This standard asks students to assess the advantages and disadvantages of using certain types of presentation mechanisms over others. With this graphic organizer, students are able to write the topic/idea at the top and evaluate each medium's advantages in the middle column and disadvantages in the right column.

## Topic/Idea:

| Medium | Advantages | Disadvantages |
|---|---|---|
| **Print/ Digital Text** | | |
| **Video** | | |
| **Multi- media** | | |

## CCSS.ELA-Literacy.RI.8.8

Delineate and evaluate the argument and specific claims in a text, assessing whether the reasoning is sound and the evidence is relevant and sufficient; recognize when irrelevant evidence is introduced.*

## Explanation

This standard asks students to outline and assess an informational author's argument or claim in terms of reasons and evidence and identify irrelevant evidence. With this graphic organizer, students are able to write the author's argument or claim in the top box, delineate and evaluate reasons in the second row, delineate and evaluate relevant evidence in the third row, and delineate irrelevant evidence in the fourth row.

### Argument/Claim

| | |
|---|---|
| | |

| Delineation | Evaluation |
|---|---|
| Reasons- | Soundness of Reasons- |
| Relevant Evidence- | Sufficiency of Evidence- |
| Irrelevant Evidence- | |

## CCSS.ELA-Literacy.RI.8.9

Analyze a case in which two or more texts provide conflicting information on the same topic and identify where the texts disagree on matters of fact or interpretation.*

## Explanation

This standard asks students to examine the differences of various informational texts that are written on the same topic, yet presented differently. With this graphic organizer, students are able to write the topic at the top and text names in the first row, determine conflicting information for both texts in the second row, and, based on that, identify where the texts disagree on matters of fact or interpretation in the third row.

**Topic:**

|  | Text 1: | Text 2: |
|---|---|---|
| **Conflicting Information** |  |  |
| **Choose One and Explain: Disagreement of Fact or Interpretation** |  |  |

## CCSS.ELA-Literacy.RI.8.10

By the end of the year, read and comprehend literary nonfiction at the high end of the grades 6–8 text complexity band independently and proficiently.*

## Explanation

This standard asks students to read nonfiction texts that are grade-level appropriate. No table or graphic organizer is applicable.

# CHAPTER 12

# 8th Grade
# Reading Literature Text

# CCSS.ELA-Literacy.RL.8.1

Cite the textual evidence that most strongly supports an analysis of what the text says explicitly as well as inferences drawn from the text.*

## Explanation

This standard asks students to indicate the most powerful proof of explicit and inferential meaning within a literature text. With this graphic organizer, students are able to analyze for explicit and inferential meaning in the top row, relate various pieces of evidence for those individual meanings in the middle row, and explain the strongest piece of evidence in the bottom row.

| Explicit Meaning | |
|---|---|
| Textual Evidence | -<br>-<br>- |
| Which Evidence is the Strongest? Why? | |

| Inferential Meaning | |
|---|---|
| Textual Evidence | -<br>-<br>- |
| Which Evidence is the Strongest? Why? | |

# CCSS.ELA-Literacy.RL.8.2

Determine a theme or central idea of a text and analyze its development over the course of the text, including its relationship to the characters, setting, and plot; provide an objective summary of the text.*

## Explanation

This standard asks students to establish the essential idea/theme and how it connects to the characters, setting, and plot within a literature text, then summarize. With this graphic organizer, students are able to express the central idea/theme in the box at the top and relate how it connects to the characters, setting, and plot in the small boxes. Space is provided for a summary as well.

## Central Idea/Theme

| | | |
|---|---|---|
| **Characters** | **Setting** | **Plot** |
| **Characters** | **Setting** | **Plot** |

## Summary:

_____

_____

_____

_____

_____

_____

_____

# CCSS.ELA-Literacy.RL.8.3

Analyze how particular lines of dialogue or incidents in a story or drama propel the action, reveal aspects of a character, or provoke a decision.*

## Explanation

This standard asks students to examine how a story's characters' discourse or situations relate to plot or characterization. With this graphic organizer, students are able to document the dialogue or incident in the left column and relate how it propels the action, reveals aspects of a character, or provokes a decision in the right column.

| Dialogue/Incident | Analysis (Choose One to Explain: Propel the action, Reveal aspects of a character, Provoke a decision) |
|---|---|
|  |  |

| Dialogue/Incident | Analysis (Choose One to Explain: Propel the action, Reveal aspects of a character, Provoke a decision) |
|---|---|
|  |  |

# CCSS.ELA-Literacy.RL.8.4

Determine the meaning of words and phrases as they are used in a text, including figurative and connotative meanings; analyze the impact of specific word choices on meaning and tone, including analogies or allusions to other texts.*

# Explanation

This standard asks students to establish different meanings for words and phrases in a literature text and determine the relation of specific word choices on meaning and tone. With this graphic organizer, students are able to use the left table to write the word or phrase in the first column and describe its various definitions in the second column. Students are able to use the right table to write a specific word choice in the first column and analyze its impact on meaning and tone in the second column.

| Word/ Phrase | Definition |
|---|---|
| | Figurative- |
| | Connotative- |

| Specific Word Choice | Impact Analysis |
|---|---|
| Analogies- | Meaning- |
| Allusions to Other Texts- | Tone- |

## CCSS.ELA-Literacy.RL.8.5

Compare and contrast the structure of two or more texts and analyze how the differing structure of each text contributes to its meaning and style.*

## Explanation

This standard asks students to note the structural similarities and differences of two or more literary texts and determine how the text structures add to meaning and style. With this graphic organizer, students are able to write the texts' names at the top, identify structural differences in the non-intersecting parts of the circles and identify structural similarities in the intersection of the two circles. Students are able to explain how the different structure of each text contributes to its meaning and style in the boxes on the left.

**How the Different Structure of Each Text Contributes to its Meaning and Style**

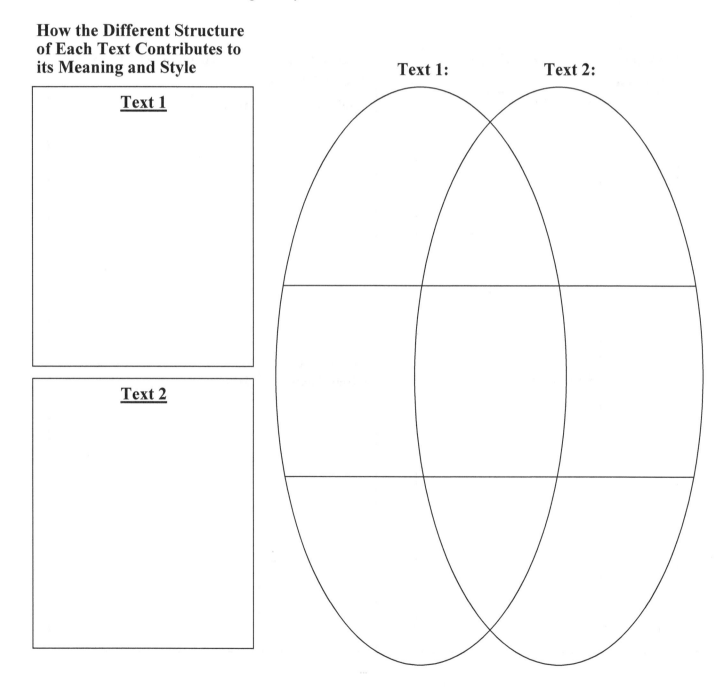

**Text 1**

**Text 2**

Text 1:

Text 2:

# CCSS.ELA-Literacy.RL.8.6

Analyze how differences in the points of view of the characters and the audience or reader (e.g., created through the use of dramatic irony) create such effects as suspense or humor.*

## Explanation

This standard asks students to note how the differences in points of view of the characters and the audience/reader produce suspense or humor. With this graphic organizer, students are able to write the different points of view in the corresponding circles. Then, based on that, students are able to explain how those differing points of view create suspense or humor in the box on the left.

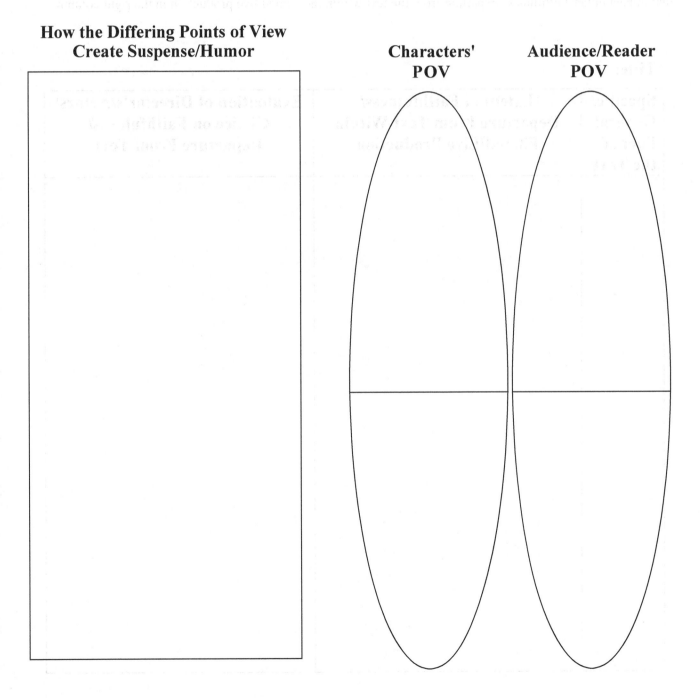

# CCSS.ELA-Literacy.RL.8.7

Analyze the extent to which a filmed or live production of a story or drama stays faithful to or departs from the text or script, evaluating the choices made by the director or actors.*

## Explanation

This standard asks students to examine the degree of similarity or difference between a literary text and its theatrical interpretation and evaluate related choices made by the director or actors. With this graphic organizer, students are able to write the title at the top, identify a part of the text in the left column, relate the extent of its faithfulness or departure within filmed/live production in the middle column, and evaluate the choices of the director/actors that impact either faithfulness/departure from the text within the filmed/live production in the right column.

**Title:**

| Specific/ General Part of the Text | Extent of Faithfulness/ Departure From Text Within Filmed/Live Production | Evaluation of Director's/Actors' Choice on Faithfulness/ Departure From Text |
|---|---|---|
| | | |

# CCSS.ELA-Literacy.RL.8.9

Analyze how a modern work of fiction draws on themes, patterns of events, or character types from myths, traditional stories, or religious works such as the Bible, including describing how the material is rendered new.*

# Explanation

This standard asks students to examine how modern fiction utilizes themes, patterns of events, or character types of myths, traditional stories, or religious works and describe how modern fiction recycles the three elements. With this graphic organizer, students are able to write the name of the texts in the first row of columns one and two, note the themes, patterns of events, or character types within a work of modern fiction in the left column, relate themes, patterns of events, or character types within a myth, traditional story, or religious work in the middle column, and explain how modern fiction is rendered new in the right column.

| Modern Fiction: | Historical Work: | How the Material is Rendered New |
|---|---|---|
| Themes- | Themes- | |
| Event Patterns- | Event Patterns- | |
| Character Types- | Character Types- | |

## CCSS.ELA-Literacy.RL.8.10

By the end of the year, read and comprehend literature, including stories, dramas, and poems, at the high end of grades 6–8 text complexity band independently and proficiently.*

## Explanation

This standard asks students to read literature texts that are grade-level appropriate. No table or graphic organizer is applicable.

# CHAPTER 13

# 8th Grade Writing

## CCSS.ELA-Literacy.W.8.1

Write arguments to support claims with clear reasons and relevant evidence.*

## CCSS.ELA-Literacy.W.8.1.a

Introduce claim(s), acknowledge and distinguish the claim(s) from alternate or opposing claims, and organize the reasons and evidence logically.*

## CCSS.ELA-Literacy.W.8.1.b

Support claim(s) with logical reasoning and relevant evidence, using accurate, credible sources and demonstrating an understanding of the topic or text.*

## Explanation

This group of standards asks students to write to persuade through the use of claims, reasons, and evidence, while recognizing and distinguishing a counter claim. With this graphic organizer, students are able to brainstorm a claim/alternate claim in the top table, make a distinction between them in the top table, and brainstorm reasons, evidence, and sources in the bottom table.

| Claim | Alternate Claim | Distinction between Claims |
|---|---|---|
|  |  |  |

| Support | Support | Support |
|---|---|---|
| Reason 1- | Reason 2- | Reason 3- |
| Evidence 1- | Evidence 2- | Evidence 3- |
| Source- | Source- | Source- |
| Is it credible?- | Is it credible?- | Is it credible?- |

## CCSS.ELA-Literacy.W.8.1

Write arguments to support claims with clear reasons and relevant evidence.*

## CCSS.ELA-Literacy.W.8.1.c

Use words, phrases, and clauses to create cohesion and clarify the relationships among claim(s), counterclaims, reasons, and evidence.*

## Explanation

This standard asks students to use particular language to associate claim, counterclaim, reasons, and evidence within persuasive writing. With this graphic organizer, students are able to use the top table to write the claim in the left column, write reasons in the middle column, and brainstorm words, phrases, and/or clauses that create cohesion and clarify the relationship among them in the right column. Students are able to use the middle table to write reasons in the left column, write evidence in the middle column, and brainstorm words, phrases, and/or clauses that create cohesion and clarify the relationship among them in the right column. Students are able to use the bottom table to write a claim in the first column, write a counterclaim in the second column, and brainstorm words, phrases, and/or clauses that create cohesion and clarify the relationship among them in the third column.

| Claim | Reasons | | Words/Phrases/Clauses That Clarify |
|---|---|---|---|
| | 1 | | |
| | 2 | | |
| | 3 | | |

| Reasons | Evidence | Words/Phrases/Clauses That Clarify |
|---|---|---|
| 1 | 1 | |
| 2 | 2 | |
| 3 | 3 | |

| Claim | Counterclaim | Words/Phrases/Clauses That Clarify |
|---|---|---|
| | | |

# CCSS.ELA-Literacy.W.8.1

Write arguments to support claims with clear reasons and relevant evidence.*

# CCSS.ELA-Literacy.W.8.1.d

Establish and maintain a formal style.*

# Explanation

This standard asks students to have a formal writing style within persuasive writing. Because this standard leaves room for a teacher's interpretation, this example guide allows for modeling and guided practice so that students understand the difference between formal and informal writing styles.

## Informal Writing Style:

_____

_____

_____

_____

_____

_____

_____

_____

## Formal Writing Style:

_____

_____

_____

_____

_____

_____

_____

_____

## CCSS.ELA-Literacy.W.8.1

Write arguments to support claims with clear reasons and relevant evidence.*

## CCSS.ELA-Literacy.W.8.1.e

Provide a concluding statement or section that follows from and supports the argument presented.*

## Explanation

This standard asks students to write a conclusion for persuasive writing. With this graphic organizer, students are able to write claim, reasons, and/or evidence in the top three boxes and, based on that, brainstorm a logical conclusion in the bottom box.

| Claim/Reason/ Evidence 1 | Claim/Reason/ Evidence 2 | Claim/Reason/ Evidence 3 |
|---|---|---|
|  |  |  |

**Conclusion**

## CCSS.ELA-Literacy.W.8.2

Write informative/explanatory texts to examine a topic and convey ideas, concepts, and information through the selection, organization, and analysis of relevant content.*

## CCSS.ELA-Literacy.W.8.2.a

Introduce a topic clearly, previewing what is to follow; organize ideas, concepts, and information into broader categories; include formatting (e.g., headings), graphics (e.g., charts, tables), and multimedia when useful to aiding comprehension.*

## Explanation

This standard asks students to utilize the elements of introduction, organization/broader categories, formatting, and graphics/multimedia for informative/explanatory writing. With this graphic organizer, students are able to write the topic at the top and brainstorm an introduction in the first table, an organization strategy/categorization in the second table, formatting in the third table, and graphics/multimedia in the fourth table.

**Topic:**

| Introduction | |
|---|---|
| | |

| Organization/Categorization |
|---|
| |

| Formatting<br>(Headings) |
|---|
| |

| Graphics/Multimedia<br>(Charts, Tables) |
|---|
| |

## CCSS.ELA-Literacy.W.8.2

Write informative/explanatory texts to examine a topic and convey ideas, concepts, and information through the selection, organization, and analysis of relevant content.*

## CCSS.ELA-Literacy.W.8.2.b

Develop the topic with relevant, well-chosen facts, definitions, concrete details, quotations, or other information and examples.*

## Explanation

This standard asks students to have the micro elements of appropriate facts, definitions, details, quotations, and examples within informative/explanatory writing. With this graphic organizer, students are able to write the topic at the top and brainstorm these elements inside.

**Topic:**

| Development |
|---|
| **Well-Chosen Facts-** |
| **Definitions-** |
| **Concrete Details-** |
| **Quotations-** |
| **Other Information/Examples-** |

## CCSS.ELA-Literacy.W.8.2

Write informative/explanatory texts to examine a topic and convey ideas, concepts, and information through the selection, organization, and analysis of relevant content.*

## CCSS.ELA-Literacy.W.8.2.c

Use appropriate and varied transitions to create cohesion and clarify the relationships among ideas and concepts.*

## Explanation

This standard asks students to use particular language to associate ideas and concepts within informative/explanatory writing. With this graphic organizer, students are able to write their ideas and concepts in the left table and brainstorm transitions that create cohesion and clarify how they relate in the right boxes.

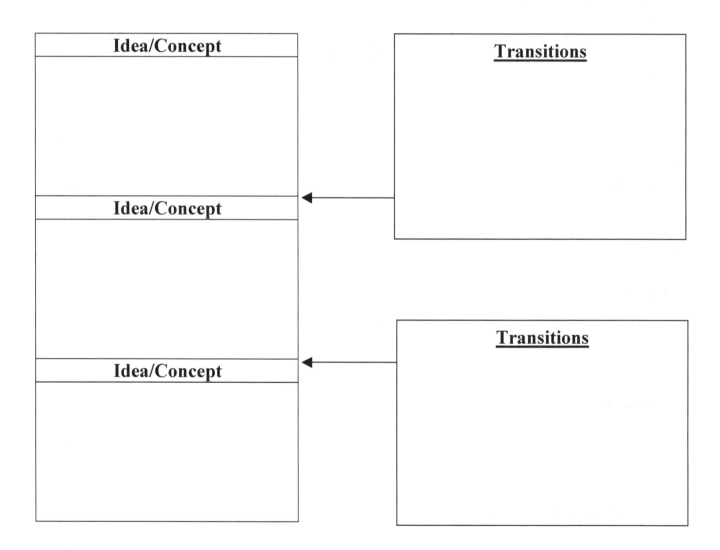

## CCSS.ELA-Literacy.W.8.2

Write informative/explanatory texts to examine a topic and convey ideas, concepts, and information through the selection, organization, and analysis of relevant content.*

## CCSS.ELA-Literacy.W.8.2.d

Use precise language and domain-specific vocabulary to inform about or explain the topic.*

## Explanation

This standard asks students to utilize certain subject matter words within informative/explanatory writing. With this graphic organizer, students are able to write the topic at the top and brainstorm precise domain-specific vocabulary that relates to the topic inside.

**Topic:**

| Precise/Domain-Specific Vocabulary |
|---|
|  |

# CCSS.ELA-Literacy.W.8.2

Write informative/explanatory texts to examine a topic and convey ideas, concepts, and information through the selection, organization, and analysis of relevant content.*

# CCSS.ELA-Literacy.W.8.2.e

Establish and maintain a formal style.*

# Explanation

This standard asks students to have a formal writing style within informative/explanatory writing. Because this standard leaves room for a teacher's interpretation, this example guide allows for modeling and guided practice so that students understand the difference between formal and informal writing styles.

## Informal Writing Style:

_____

_____

_____

_____

_____

_____

_____

## Formal Writing Style:

_____

_____

_____

_____

_____

_____

_____

## CCSS.ELA-Literacy.W.8.2

Write informative/explanatory texts to examine a topic and convey ideas, concepts, and information through the selection, organization, and analysis of relevant content.*

## CCSS.ELA-Literacy.W.8.2.f

Provide a concluding statement or section that follows from and supports the information or explanation presented.*

## Explanation

This standard asks students to write a conclusion for informative/explanatory writing. With this graphic organizer, students are able to write concepts or ideas presented in the top three boxes and, based on that, brainstorm a logical conclusion in the bottom box.

| Concept/Idea 1 | Concept/Idea 2 | Concept/Idea 3 |
|---|---|---|
| | | |

**Conclusion**

# CCSS.ELA-Literacy.W.8.3

Write narratives to develop real or imagined experiences or events using effective technique, relevant descriptive details, and well-structured event sequences.*

# CCSS.ELA-Literacy.W.8.3.a

Engage and orient the reader by establishing a context and point of view and introducing a narrator and/or characters; organize an event sequence that unfolds naturally and logically.*

# CCSS.ELA-Literacy.W.8.3.b

Use narrative techniques, such as dialogue, pacing, description, and reflection, to develop experiences, events, and/or characters.*

# CCSS.ELA-Literacy.W.8.3.d

Use precise words and phrases, relevant descriptive details, and sensory language to capture the action and convey experiences and events.*

# Explanation

This group of standards asks students to have the macro elements of context, characters, point of view, and event sequence and micro elements of dialogue, pacing, description, reflection, precise language, relevant descriptive details, and sensory language that develop experiences, events, and/or characters in narrative writing. With this graphic organizer, students are able to brainstorm these elements, making sure they relate to each other.

## Establish

| |
|---|
| **Context:** |
| **Characters/Narrator:** |
| **Point of View:** |

## Event Sequence

| Event 1 | Narrative Technique (Choose):<br>Dialogue, Pacing, Reflection, or Description | To Develop (Choose): |
|---------|------------------------------------------------------------------------------|----------------------|
| | precise words and phrases, relevant descriptive details, and sensory language: | Events, Experiences, or Characters |

*Continued on next page

| Event 2 | **Narrative Technique (Choose):**<br>Dialogue, Pacing, Reflection, or Description | **To Develop (Choose):** |
|---|---|---|
| | precise words and phrases, relevant descriptive details, and sensory language: | Events, Experiences, or Characters |

| Event 3 | **Narrative Technique (Choose):**<br>Dialogue, Pacing, Reflection, or Description | **To Develop (Choose):** |
|---|---|---|
| | precise words and phrases, relevant descriptive details, and sensory language: | Events, Experiences, or Characters |

| Event 4 | **Narrative Technique (Choose):**<br>Dialogue, Pacing, Reflection, or Description | **To Develop (Choose):** |
|---|---|---|
| | precise words and phrases, relevant descriptive details, and sensory language: | Events, Experiences, or Characters |

| Event 5 | **Narrative Technique (Choose):**<br>Dialogue, Pacing, Reflection, or Description | **To Develop (Choose):** |
|---|---|---|
| | precise words and phrases, relevant descriptive details, and sensory language: | Events, Experiences, or Characters |

## CCSS.ELA-Literacy.W.8.3

Write narratives to develop real or imagined experiences or events using effective technique, relevant descriptive details, and well-structured event sequences.*

## CCSS.ELA-Literacy.W.8.3.c

Use a variety of transition words, phrases, and clauses to convey sequence, signal shifts from one time frame or setting to another, and show the relationships among experiences and events.*

## Explanation

This standard asks students to use particular language to express time progression within narrative writing. With this graphic organizer, students are able to write events in the left table and brainstorm words, phrases, and clauses that convey sequence and signal shifts from one time frame or setting to another in the right boxes.

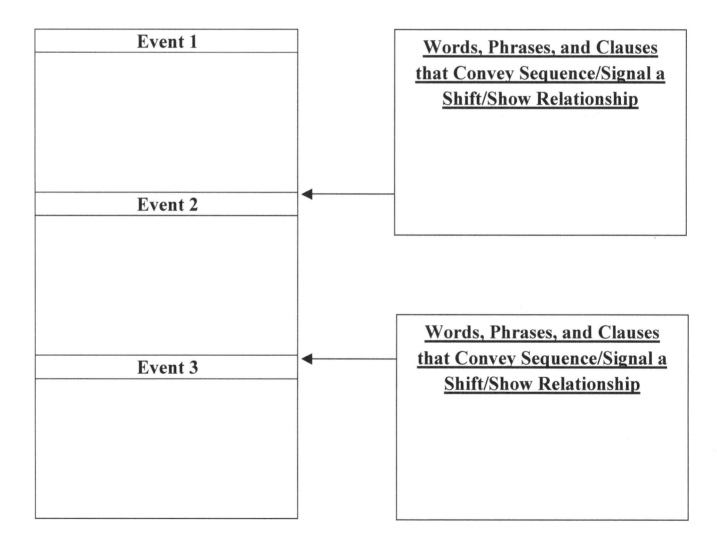

## CCSS.ELA-Literacy.W.8.3

Write narratives to develop real or imagined experiences or events using effective technique, relevant descriptive details, and well-structured event sequences.*

## CCSS.ELA-Literacy.W.8.3.e

Provide a conclusion that follows from and reflects on the narrated experiences or events.*

## Explanation

This standard asks students to write a conclusion for narrative writing. With this graphic organizer, students are able to write experiences or events of the narrative in the top three boxes and, based on that, brainstorm a logical conclusion in the bottom box.

| Event/Experience 1 | Event/Experience 2 | Event/Experience 3 |
|---|---|---|
| | | |

**Conclusion**

# CCSS.ELA-Literacy.W.8.4

Produce clear and coherent writing in which the development, organization, and style are appropriate to task, purpose, and audience. (Grade-specific expectations for writing types are defined in standards 1–3 above.)*

# Explanation

This standard asks students to have clear/coherent writing for persuasive, informative/explanatory, and narrative texts. Because this standard leaves room for a teacher's interpretation, this example guide allows for modeling and guided practice so that students understand the difference between unclear/incoherent and clear/coherent writing styles.

## Unclear/Incoherent Writing Style:

_____

_____

_____

_____

_____

_____

_____

## Clear/Coherent Writing Style:

_____

_____

_____

_____

_____

_____

_____

## CCSS.ELA-Literacy.W.8.5

With some guidance and support from peers and adults, develop and strengthen writing as needed by planning, revising, editing, rewriting, or trying a new approach, focusing on how well purpose and audience have been addressed. (Editing for conventions should demonstrate command of Language standards 1–3 up to and including grade 8 here.)*

## Explanation

This standard asks students to use the writing process for persuasive, informative/explanatory, and narrative texts. No table or graphic organizer is applicable.

## <u>CCSS.ELA-Literacy.W.8.6</u>

Use technology, including the Internet, to produce and publish writing and present the relationships between information and ideas efficiently as well as to interact and collaborate with others.*

## <u>Explanation</u>

This standard asks students to use technology for persuasive, informative/explanatory, and narrative texts. No table or graphic organizer is applicable.

## CCSS.ELA-Literacy.W.8.7

Conduct short research projects to answer a question (including a self-generated question), drawing on several sources and generating additional related, focused questions that allow for multiple avenues of exploration.*

## Explanation

This standard asks students to find information from various sources for research writing and create questions connected to the research question. With this graphic organizer, students are able to write the research question at the top, identify information from various sources in the big boxes, make sure it is related to their research question at the top, and identify additional related, focused questions that allow for multiple avenues of exploration in the small boxes.

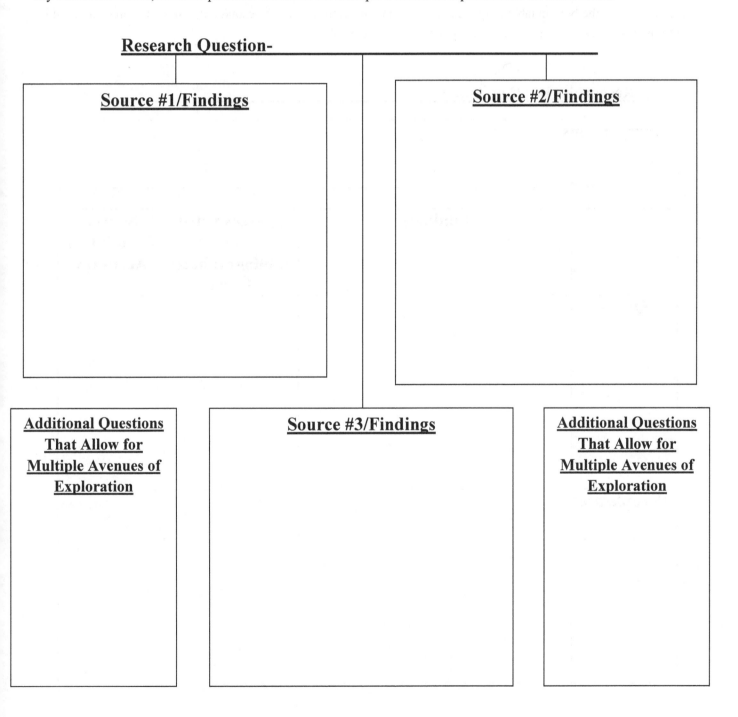

## CCSS.ELA-Literacy.W.8.8

Gather relevant information from multiple print and digital sources, using search terms effectively; assess the credibility and accuracy of each source; and quote or paraphrase the data and conclusions of others while avoiding plagiarism and following a standard format for citation.*

## Explanation

This standard asks students to find pertinent information, utilize searches, evaluate the value of the information, quote/paraphrase the information without plagiarism, and cite sources. With this graphic organizer, students are able to use the top table to write the research question/topic at the top and brainstorm related search terms inside. Students are able to use the bottom table to quote and/or paraphrase findings in the second column, cite sources in the third column, and assess credibility of those sources in the fourth column.

### Research Question/Topic-

**Search Terms:**

|  | Findings | Sources Cited in Bibliographical Form | Source Credibility/ Accuracy |
|---|---|---|---|
| **Quote** |  |  |  |
| **Paraphrase** |  |  |  |

## CCSS.ELA-Literacy.W.8.9

Draw evidence from literary or informational texts to support analysis, reflection, and research.*

## CCSS.ELA-Literacy.W.8.9.a

Apply *grade 8 Reading standards* to literature (e.g., "Analyze how a modern work of fiction draws on themes, patterns of events, or character types from myths, traditional stories, or religious works such as the Bible, including describing how the material is rendered new").*

## CCSS.ELA-Literacy.W.8.9.b

Apply *grade 8 Reading standards* to literary nonfiction (e.g., "Delineate and evaluate the argument and specific claims in a text, assessing whether the reasoning is sound and the evidence is relevant and sufficient; recognize when irrelevant evidence is introduced").*

## Explanation

This group of standards asks students to write for the purpose of expressing the reading standards. With the first example guide, students are able to link a literature reading standard at the top to related analysis, reflection, and research below it. With the second example guide, students are able to link a literary nonfiction reading standard at the top to related analysis, reflection, and research below it.

**Literature Standard:**_____

**Analysis/Reflection/Research:**

_____

_____

_____

_____

_____


**Nonfiction Standard:**_____

**Analysis/Reflection/Research:**

_____

_____

_____

_____

_____

## <u>CCSS.ELA-Literacy.W.8.10</u>

Write routinely over extended time frames (time for research, reflection, and revision) and shorter time frames (a single sitting or a day or two) for a range of discipline-specific tasks, purposes, and audiences.*

## <u>Explanation</u>

This standard asks students to write short and long pieces of writing. No table or graphic organizer is applicable.

# CHAPTER 14

# 8th Grade
# Speaking/Listening

## CCSS.ELA-Literacy.SL.8.1

Engage effectively in a range of collaborative discussions (one-on-one, in groups, and teacher-led) with diverse partners on grade 8 topics, texts, and issues, building on others' ideas and expressing their own clearly.*

## CCSS.ELA-Literacy.SL.8.1.a

Come to discussions prepared, having read or researched material under study; explicitly draw on that preparation by referring to evidence on the topic, text, or issue to probe and reflect on ideas under discussion.*

## Explanation

This standard asks students to be ready with topical evidence for class discussions. With this graphic organizer, students are able write the topic/text/issue at the top and prepare using an outline, a graphic organizer, or both.

### Topic/Text/Issue of Discussion:

| Evidence From Reading/Studying: | Evidence From Reading/Studying: |
|---|---|
| I.<br>A.<br>B.<br>C.<br><br>II.<br>A.<br>B.<br>C.<br><br>III.<br>A.<br>B.<br>C.<br><br>IV.<br>A.<br>B.<br>C.<br><br>V.<br>A.<br>B.<br>C. | |

## CCSS.ELA-Literacy.SL.8.1

Engage effectively in a range of collaborative discussions (one-on-one, in groups, and teacher-led) with diverse partners on grade 8 topics, texts, and issues, building on others' ideas and expressing their own clearly.*

## CCSS.ELA-Literacy.SL.8.1.b

Follow rules for collegial discussions and decision-making, track progress toward specific goals and deadlines, and define individual roles as needed.*

## Explanation

This standard asks students to participate in setting and tracking class discussion norms. With this graphic organizer, students are able to write the topic/issue at the top, propose rules, goals, deadlines, and roles in the middle column, and track their progress in the right column.

### Topic/Issue of Discussion:

| Rules | | Progress Check/Reflection: |
|---|---|---|
| Goals | | Progress Check/Reflection: |
| Deadlines | | Progress Check/Reflection: |
| Individual Roles | | Progress Check/Reflection: |

## CCSS.ELA-Literacy.SL.8.1

Engage effectively in a range of collaborative discussions (one-on-one, in groups, and teacher-led) with diverse partners on grade 8 topics, texts, and issues, building on others' ideas and expressing their own clearly.*

## CCSS.ELA-Literacy.SL.8.1.c

Pose questions that connect the ideas of several speakers and respond to others' questions and comments with relevant evidence, observations, and ideas.*

## Explanation

This standard asks students to participate in class discussion with questions that relate the ideas of various speakers and responses to others' questions/comments with proof, observations, and thoughts. With this graphic organizer, students are able to use the top table to write the topic/issue at the top, capture ideas of other speakers in the left column and document their own questions in the right column. Students are able to use the bottom table to capture questions/comments from others in the left column and document their own responses in the right column.

**Topic/Issue of Discussion:**

| Ideas of Other Speakers | My Questions (That Connect Ideas of Speakers) |
|---|---|
|  |  |

| Questions/Comments From Others | My Responses (Using Evidence/Observations/Ideas) |
|---|---|
|  |  |

## CCSS.ELA-Literacy.SL.8.1

Engage effectively in a range of collaborative discussions (one-on-one, in groups, and teacher-led) with diverse partners on grade 8 topics, texts, and issues, building on others' ideas and expressing their own clearly.*

## CCSS.ELA-Literacy.SL.8.1.d

Acknowledge new information expressed by others, and, when warranted, qualify or justify their own views in light of the evidence presented.*

## Explanation

This standard asks students to recognize new knowledge communicated in class discussions and defend their perspective based on that. With this graphic organizer, students are able to write the topic/issue and their view at the top, record new information expressed by others in the left column, and qualify/justify their views in the right column.

## Topic/Issue of Discussion:

**Your View:**

_____

_____

_____

| Information Expressed by Others | Qualification/Justification of Your Views |
|---|---|
|  |  |
|  |  |
|  |  |

# CCSS.ELA-Literacy.SL.8.2

Analyze the purpose of information presented in diverse media and formats (e.g., visually, quantitatively, orally) and evaluate the motives (e.g., social, commercial, political) behind its presentation.*

# Explanation

This standard asks students to examine the rationale for various types of given material and assess the reasons for their use. With this graphic organizer, students are able to write the topic/issue at the top, identify the purpose of using particular presentation media/format in the left column, and evaluate the various motives behind presenting in that media/format in the right column.

## Topic/Issue of Presentation:

| Purpose of Media/Format | Motive Evaluation (Choose: social, commercial, political) |
|---|---|
| **Visual Information:** | |
| **Quantitative Information:** | |
| **Oral Information:** | |

# CCSS.ELA-Literacy.SL.8.3

Delineate a speaker's argument and specific claims, evaluating the soundness of the reasoning and relevance and sufficiency of the evidence and identifying when irrelevant evidence is introduced.*

## Explanation

This standard asks students to outline and assess a speaker's argument or claim in terms of reasons and evidence and identify irrelevant evidence. With this graphic organizer, students are able to write the speaker's argument or claim in the top box, delineate and evaluate reasons in the second row, delineate and evaluate relevant evidence in the third row, and delineate irrelevant evidence in the fourth row.

## Argument/Claim

| Delineation | Evaluation |
|---|---|
| Reasons- | Soundness of Reasons- |
| Relevant Evidence- | Sufficiency of Evidence- |
| Irrelevant Evidence- | |

# CCSS.ELA-Literacy.SL.8.4

Present claims and findings, emphasizing salient points in a focused, coherent manner with relevant evidence, sound valid reasoning, and well-chosen details; use appropriate eye contact, adequate volume, and clear pronunciation.*

## Explanation

This standard asks students to present findings or claims in terms of connected, well-chosen reasons and evidence. With this graphic organizer, students are able to write the claim/finding in the top box and emphasize salient points through reasons/evidence/well-chosen details in the bottom box.

## Claim/Finding

|  |
|  |

↓

## Salient Points

**Sound Valid Reasons-**

**Relevant Evidence-**

**Well Chosen Details-**

## CCSS.ELA-Literacy.SL.8.5

Integrate multimedia and visual displays into presentations to clarify information, strengthen claims and evidence, and add interest.*

## Explanation

This standard asks students to be ready for class speeches by combining interactive media elements and visuals in a strategic manner. With this graphic organizer, students are able to brainstorm what they intend to present in the left column, relate what multimedia/visuals could be utilized in the middle column, and explain how the multimedia/visuals clarify information, strengthen claims/evidence, and add interest in the right column.

| Presentation Information (Main Ideas) | Possible Multimedia/Visual Components | How the Multimedia/Visual Component Clarifies/Strengthens/Adds Interest |
|---|---|---|
| | | |
| | | |
| | | |

## CCSS.ELA-Literacy.SL.8.6

Adapt speech to a variety of contexts and tasks, demonstrating command of formal English when indicated or appropriate. (See grade 8 Language standards 1 and 3 here for specific expectations.)*

## Explanation

This standard asks students to speak within a range of grade-level situations. No table or graphic organizer is applicable.

# CHAPTER 15
# 8th Grade Language

*The Visual Edge©*

## CCSS.ELA-Literacy.L.8.1

Demonstrate command of the conventions of standard English grammar and usage when writing or speaking.*

## CCSS.ELA-Literacy.L.8.1.a

Explain the function of verbals (gerunds, participles, infinitives) in general and their function in particular sentences.*

## Explanation

This standard asks students to clarify the purpose of gerunds, participles, and infinitives. With this graphic organizer, students are able to write a particular verbal in the left column, use it in a sentence in the middle column, and explain its function in the right column.

| Gerund/ Participle/ Infinitive | Sentence Example | Explanation |
|---|---|---|
| | | **General Function-**<br><br>**Specific Function in Example-** |
| | | **General Function-**<br><br>**Specific Function in Example-** |
| | | **General Function-**<br><br>**Specific Function in Example-** |

## CCSS.ELA-Literacy.L.8.1

Demonstrate command of the conventions of standard English grammar and usage when writing or speaking.*

## CCSS.ELA-Literacy.L.8.1.b

Form and use verbs in the active and passive voice.*

## Explanation

This standard asks students to utilize active and passive voice verbs. With this example guide, students are given space to discern the difference between sentences with verbs in active and passive voice.

**Active:**

_____

**Passive:**

_____

**Active:**

_____

**Passive:**

_____

**Active:**

_____

**Passive:**

_____

**Active:**

_____

**Passive:**

_____

# CCSS.ELA-Literacy.L.8.1

Demonstrate command of the conventions of standard English grammar and usage when writing or speaking.*

# CCSS.ELA-Literacy.L.8.1.c

Form and use verbs in the indicative, imperative, interrogative, conditional, and subjunctive mood.*

# Explanation

This standard asks students to utilize different types of verb moods. With this example guide, students are given space to discern the difference between sentences that contain the five verb moods.

**Indicative:**

_____

**Imperative:**

_____

**Interrogative:**

_____

**Conditional:**

_____

**Subjunctive:**

_____

**Indicative:**

_____

**Imperative:**

_____

**Interrogative:**

_____

**Conditional:**

_____

**Subjunctive:**

_____

# CCSS.ELA-Literacy.L.8.1

Demonstrate command of the conventions of standard English grammar and usage when writing or speaking.*

# CCSS.ELA-Literacy.L.8.1.d

Recognize and correct inappropriate shifts in verb voice and mood.*

# Explanation

This standard asks students to notice mistakes in and rectify verb voice and mood. With this example guide, students are given space to discern the difference between sentences with appropriate and inappropriate verb voice and mood.

**Inappropriate Verb Voice/Mood:**

_____

**Corrected/Appropriate Verb Voice/Mood:**

_____

**Inappropriate Verb Voice/Mood:**

_____

**Corrected/Appropriate Verb Voice/Mood:**

_____

**Inappropriate Verb Voice/Mood:**

_____

**Corrected/Appropriate Verb Voice/Mood:**

_____

**Inappropriate Verb Voice/Mood:**

_____

**Corrected/Appropriate Verb Voice/Mood:**

_____

*The Visual Edge*©

## CCSS.ELA-Literacy.L.8.2

Demonstrate command of the conventions of standard English capitalization, punctuation, and spelling when writing.*

## CCSS.ELA-Literacy.L.8.2.a

Use punctuation (comma, ellipsis, dash) to indicate a pause or break.*

## Explanation

This standard asks students to utilize a comma, ellipsis, and dash to specify a stoppage in a sentence. With this example guide, students are given space to discern the difference between the three types of punctuation that can be used to indicate a pause or break in a sentence.

**Comma:**

_____

**Ellipsis:**

_____

**Dash:**

_____

**Comma:**

_____

**Ellipsis:**

_____

**Dash:**

_____

**Comma:**

_____

**Ellipsis:**

_____

**Dash:**

_____

## CCSS.ELA-LITERACY.L.8.2

Demonstrate command of the conventions of standard English capitalization, punctuation, and spelling when writing.*

## CCSS.ELA-LIERACY.L.8.2.b

Use an ellipsis to indicate an omission.*

## Explanation

This standard asks students to utilize an ellipsis to specify an omission. With this example guide, students are given space to write sentences where an ellipsis could be used to indicate an omission.

1)_____...

2)_____..._____

3)_____...

4)_____..._____

5)_____...

6)_____..._____

7)_____...

8)_____..._____

9)_____...

10)_____..._____

## CCSS.ELA-Literacy.L.8.2

Demonstrate command of the conventions of standard English capitalization, punctuation, and spelling when writing.*

## CCSS.ELA-Literacy.L.8.2.c

Spell correctly.*

## Explanation

This standard asks students to spell words precisely. No table or graphic organizer is applicable.

# CCSS.ELA-Literacy.L.8.3

Use knowledge of language and its conventions when writing, speaking, reading, or listening.*

# CCSS.ELA-Literacy.L.8.3.a

Use verbs in the active and passive voice and in the conditional and subjunctive mood to attain specific effects (e.g., emphasizing the actor or the action; expressing uncertainty or describing a state contrary to fact).*

# Explanation

This standard asks students to utilize verbs in active and passive voice and in the conditional and subjunctive mood to achieve particular reactions. With this graphic organizer, students are able to write the verb to be used in the first column, select the type of verb voice and mood to be used in the second column, choose the specific effect to be attained in the third column, and write the brainstormed sentence in the fourth column.

| Verb | Active/ Passive Voice, Conditional/ Subjunctive Mood | Specific Effect (Choose One: Emphasizing the Actor or the Action/ Expressing Uncertainty/ Describing a State Contrary to Fact) | Sentence |
|---|---|---|---|
| | | | |
| | | | |
| | | | |

## CCSS.ELA-Literacy.L.8.4

Determine or clarify the meaning of unknown and multiple-meaning words or phrases based on *grade 8 reading and content*, choosing flexibly from a range of strategies.*

## CCSS.ELA-Literacy.L.8.4.a

Use context (e.g., the overall meaning of a sentence or paragraph; a word's position or function in a sentence) as a clue to the meaning of a word or phrase.*

## Explanation

This standard asks students to utilize context for word definition clues. With this graphic organizer, students are able to write the unknown word or phrase in the left column, relate given clues to its meaning in the middle column, and make an educated guess about its definition in the right column.

| Unknown Word/Phrase | Possible Clue Words/ Overall Meaning/ Position or Function | Possible Meaning of Unknown Word/Phrase |
|---|---|---|
|  |  |  |
|  |  |  |
|  |  |  |
|  |  |  |
|  |  |  |
|  |  |  |
|  |  |  |

## CCSS.ELA-Literacy.L.8.4

Determine or clarify the meaning of unknown and multiple-meaning words or phrases based on *grade 8 reading and content*, choosing flexibly from a range of strategies.*

## CCSS.ELA-Literacy.L.8.4.b

Use common, grade-appropriate Greek or Latin affixes and roots as clues to the meaning of a word (e.g., *precede, recede, secede*).*

## Explanation

This standard asks students to utilize affixes/roots as word definition clues. With this graphic organizer, students are able to use the first table to identify affixes/roots in the first and third columns and write definitions next to each. Students are able to use the second table to write an unknown word in the left column, pick out its affix/root in the middle column, and based on the affix/root definition from the first table, make an educated guess about the unknown word's definition in the right column.

| 8th Grade Affix/Root | Definition | 8th Grade Affix/Root | Definition |
|---|---|---|---|
|  |  |  |  |
|  |  |  |  |
|  |  |  |  |
|  |  |  |  |
|  |  |  |  |
|  |  |  |  |
|  |  |  |  |
|  |  |  |  |
|  |  |  |  |
|  |  |  |  |
|  |  |  |  |

| Unknown Word | Affix/Root | Possible Definition of Unknown Word |
|---|---|---|
|  |  |  |
|  |  |  |
|  |  |  |
|  |  |  |

## CCSS.ELA-Literacy.L.8.4

Determine or clarify the meaning of unknown and multiple-meaning words or phrases based on *grade 8 reading and content*, choosing flexibly from a range of strategies.*

## CCSS.ELA-Literacy.L.8.4.c

Consult general and specialized reference materials (e.g., dictionaries, glossaries, thesauruses), both print and digital, to find the pronunciation of a word or determine or clarify its precise meaning or its part of speech.*

## Explanation

This standard asks students to utilize reference resources for unknown words. With this graphic organizer, students are able to write the unknown word in the left column and relate its definition, part of speech, and pronunciation from a reference material in the right column.

| Unknown Word | Reference Material-Definition/Part of Speech/Pronunciation |
|---|---|
|  |  |
|  |  |
|  |  |
|  |  |
|  |  |
|  |  |
|  |  |
|  |  |
|  |  |
|  |  |
|  |  |
|  |  |
|  |  |

## CCSS.ELA-Literacy.L.8.4

Determine or clarify the meaning of unknown and multiple-meaning words or phrases based on *grade 8 reading and content*, choosing flexibly from a range of strategies.*

## CCSS.ELA-Literacy.L.8.4.d

Verify the preliminary determination of the meaning of a word or phrase (e.g., by checking the inferred meaning in context or in a dictionary).*

## Explanation

This standard asks students to utilize context and dictionaries for word definition confirmation. With this graphic organizer, students are able to write the unknown word or phrase in the left column, relate its preliminary meaning in the middle column, and verify the definition in the right column.

| Word/Phrase | Preliminary Determination of Meaning | Inferred Meaning in Context/Dictionary |
|---|---|---|
|  |  |  |
|  |  |  |
|  |  |  |
|  |  |  |
|  |  |  |
|  |  |  |
|  |  |  |
|  |  |  |
|  |  |  |
|  |  |  |
|  |  |  |
|  |  |  |
|  |  |  |
|  |  |  |

# CCSS.ELA-Literacy.L.8.5

Demonstrate understanding of figurative language, word relationships, and nuances in word meanings.*

# CCSS.ELA-Literacy.L.8.5.a

Interpret figures of speech (e.g. verbal irony, puns) in context.*

# Explanation

This standard asks students to explain figures of speech. With this graphic organizer, students are able to write the figure of speech in the top row and interpret it in the bottom row.

| **Figure of Speech** (Verbal Irony, Pun) | | | |
|---|---|---|---|
| **Interpretation** | | | |

# CCSS.ELA-Literacy.L.8.5

Demonstrate understanding of figurative language, word relationships, and nuances in word meanings.*

# CCSS.ELA-Literacy.L.8.5.b

Use the relationship between particular words to better understand each of the words.*

# Explanation

This standard asks students to utilize word relationships as clues to their meaning. With this graphic organizer, students are able to write two associated words in columns one and two based on the relationship stated in the third column and explain the two associated words in the fourth column.

| Word 1 | Word 2 | Relationship | Explanation |
|--------|--------|--------------|-------------|
| | | cause/effect | 1-<br>2- |
| **Word 1** | **Word 2** | **Relationship**<br>object/function | **Explanation**<br>1-<br>2- |
| **Word 1** | **Word 2** | **Relationship**<br>item/category | **Explanation**<br>1-<br>2- |
| **Word 1** | **Word 2** | **Relationship**<br>synonym | **Explanation**<br>1-<br>2- |
| **Word 1** | **Word 2** | **Relationship**<br>antonym | **Explanation**<br>1-<br>2- |
| **Word 1** | **Word 2** | **Relationship**<br>part/whole | **Explanation**<br>1-<br>2- |

## CCSS.ELA-Literacy.L.8.5

Demonstrate understanding of figurative language, word relationships, and nuances in word meanings.*

## CCSS.ELA-Literacy.L.8.5.c

Distinguish among the connotations (associations) of words with similar denotations (definitions) (e.g., *bull-headed, willful, firm, persistent, resolute*).*

## Explanation

This standard asks students to notice the differences between the connotations and denotations of a group of words. With this graphic organizer, students are able to write similar words in the top row, relate their similar denotations in the middle row, and determine each word's connotation in the bottom row.

| Similar Words | | | |
|---|---|---|---|
| **Denotation** | | | |
| **Connotation** | | | |

| Similar Words | | | |
|---|---|---|---|
| **Denotation** | | | |
| **Connotation** | | | |

| Similar Words | | | |
|---|---|---|---|
| **Denotation** | | | |
| **Connotation** | | | |

## CCSS.ELA-Literacy.L.8.6

Acquire and use accurately grade-appropriate general academic and domain-specific words and phrases; gather vocabulary knowledge when considering a word or phrase important to comprehension or expression.*

## Explanation

This standard asks students to use vocabulary that is grade-level appropriate and collect vocabulary information. For the former, no table or graphic organizer is applicable, and the latter is addressed in CCSS.ELA-Literacy.L.8.4.

# CHAPTER 16

# 6–8th Grade
# History/Social Studies

# CCSS.ELA-Literacy.RH.6-8.1

Cite specific textual evidence to support analysis of primary and secondary sources.*

## Explanation

This standard asks students to indicate proof of examination of primary and secondary sources. With this graphic organizer, students are able to analyze in the top row and relate textual evidence in the bottom row.

| Analysis | |
|---|---|
| **Textual Evidence from Primary Source** | |

| Analysis | |
|---|---|
| **Textual Evidence from Secondary Source** | |

# CCSS.ELA-Literacy.RH.6-8.2

Determine the central ideas or information of a primary or secondary source; provide an accurate summary of the source distinct from prior knowledge or opinions.*

## Explanation

This standard asks students to identify the essential ideas of primary or secondary sources, then summarize. With this graphic organizer, students are able to write the source at the top and express the central ideas in the boxes. Space is provided for a summary as well.

**Source:**

**Central Idea**

**Central Idea**

**Central Idea**

**Central Idea**

**Summary:**

_____

_____

_____

_____

_____

_____

_____

_____

## CCSS.ELA-Literacy.RH.6-8.3

Identify key steps in a text's description of a process related to history/social studies (e.g., how a bill becomes law, how interest rates are raised or lowered).*

## Explanation

This standard asks students to chronicle a historical or social process. With this graphic organizer, students are able to write the name of the process at the top and document the process in a timeline format below.

**Name of Process:**

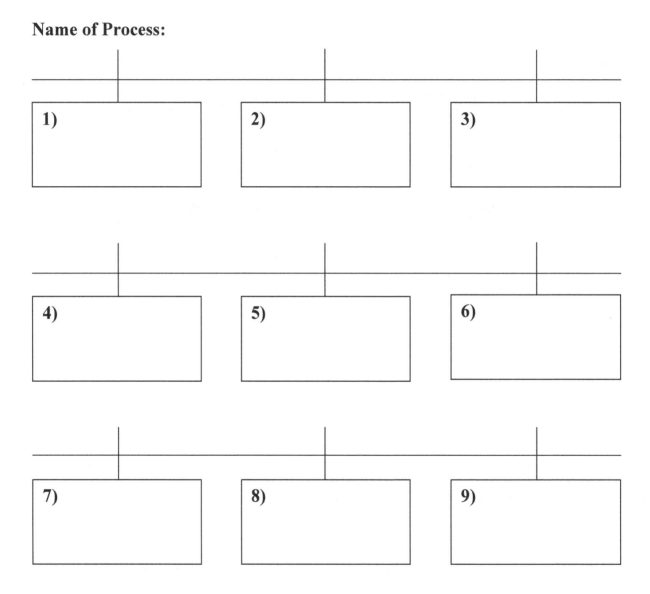

# CCSS.ELA-Literacy.RH.6-8.4

Determine the meaning of words and phrases as they are used in a text, including vocabulary specific to domains related to history/social studies.*

## Explanation

This standard asks students to establish meanings for words and phrases in a text that relate to disciplines associated with history/social studies. With this graphic organizer, students are able to write a word/phrase in the left column, identify which domain it is related to in the middle column, and establish the word's or phrase's meaning in the right column.

| Word/ Phrase | Related To (Choose: History, Politics/ Government, Sociology, Economics, or Geography) | Meaning |
|---|---|---|
|  |  |  |
|  |  |  |
|  |  |  |

## CCSS.ELA-Literacy.RH.6-8.5

Describe how a text presents information (e.g., sequentially, comparatively, causally).*

## Explanation

This standard asks students to explain how particular history/social studies information is presented in terms of style. With this graphic organizer, students are able to identify the text and its presentation style in the left column and describe how the text presents the information in the right column.

| Presentation Style | Description of How the Text Presents Information |
|---|---|
| Text:<br><br><br>(Choose One: Sequentially, Comparatively, or Causally) | |
| Text:<br><br><br>(Choose One: Sequentially, Comparatively, or Causally) | |
| Text:<br><br><br>(Choose One: Sequentially, Comparatively, or Causally) | |

# CCSS.ELA-Literacy.RH.6-8.6

Identify aspects of a text that reveal an author's point of view or purpose (e.g., loaded language, inclusion or avoidance of particular facts).*

# Explanation

This standard asks students to establish how a historical/social author demonstrates point of view or purpose through particular strategies. With this graphic organizer, students are able to determine the author's point of view in the left column and identify aspects of the text that reveal it in the right column.

| Author's Point of View/Purpose | How Point of View is Revealed |
|---|---|
| | **Loaded Language-** <br><br><br><br> **Inclusion of Facts-** <br><br><br><br> **Avoidance of Facts-** |

## CCSS.ELA-Literacy.RH.6-8.7

Integrate visual information (e.g., in charts, graphs, photographs, videos, or maps) with other information in print and digital texts.*

## Explanation

This standard asks students to combine various historical/social information. With this graphic organizer, students are able to identify various information in the top three boxes and integrate that information in the bottom box.

| __Charts/Graphs/Maps__ | __Photos/Videos__ | __Other__ |
|---|---|---|
| a.<br><br>b.<br><br>c.<br><br>d. | a.<br><br>b.<br><br>c.<br><br>d. | a.<br><br>b.<br><br>c.<br><br>d. |

__Integration__

# CCSS.ELA-Literacy.RH.6-8.8

Distinguish among fact, opinion, and reasoned judgment in a text.*

## Explanation

This standard asks students to differentiate between authentic information, a belief, and a rational decision in a historical/social text. With this graphic organizer, students are able to write the name of the text at the top and identify fact in the left column, opinion in the middle column, and reasoned judgment in the right column. Space is provided below to explain distinctions.

**Text:**

| Fact | Opinion | Reasoned Judgment |
|------|---------|-------------------|
|      |         |                   |

**Distinction Explanation:**

_____

_____

_____

_____

_____

_____

_____

## CCSS.ELA-Literacy.RH.6-8.9

Analyze the relationship between a primary and secondary source on the same topic.*

## Explanation

This standard asks students to examine the connection of a primary and secondary source on the same topic. With this graphic organizer, students are able to write the topic at the top, identify information from a primary source in the left column, identify information from a secondary source in the middle column, and explain their relationship in the right column.

**Topic:**

| Primary Source | Secondary Source | Relationship |
|---|---|---|
| | | |

## CCSS.ELA-Literacy.RH.6-8.10

By the end of grade 8, read and comprehend history/social studies texts in the grades 6–8 text complexity band independently and proficiently.*

## Explanation

This standard asks students to read historical/social texts that are grade-level appropriate. No table or graphic organizer is applicable.

# CHAPTER 17

# 6th–8th Grade Science/Technical

## CCSS.ELA-Literacy.RST.6-8.1

Cite specific textual evidence to support analysis of science and technical texts.*

## Explanation

This standard asks students to indicate proof of examination of science/technical texts. With this graphic organizer, students are able to analyze in the top row and relate evidence in the bottom row.

| Analysis | |
|---|---|
| **Textual Evidence** | |

| Analysis | |
|---|---|
| **Textual Evidence** | |

# CCSS.ELA-Literacy.RST.6-8.2

Determine the central ideas or conclusions of a text; provide an accurate summary of the text distinct from prior knowledge or opinions.*

## Explanation

This standard asks students to identify the essential ideas/conclusions of a scientific/technical text, then summarize. With this graphic organizer, students are able to express the central ideas/conclusions in the boxes. Space is provided for a summary as well.

**Central Idea/Conclusion**

**Central Idea/Conclusion**

**Central Idea/Conclusion**

**Central Idea/Conclusion**

**Summary:**

_____

_____

_____

_____

_____

_____

_____

# CCSS.ELA-Literacy.RST.6-8.3

Follow precisely a multistep procedure when carrying out experiments, taking measurements, or performing technical tasks.*

## Explanation

This standard asks students to adhere to a scientific/technical process. With this graphic organizer, students are able to write the name of the procedure at the top and document the process in a multistep format below.

**Procedure:**

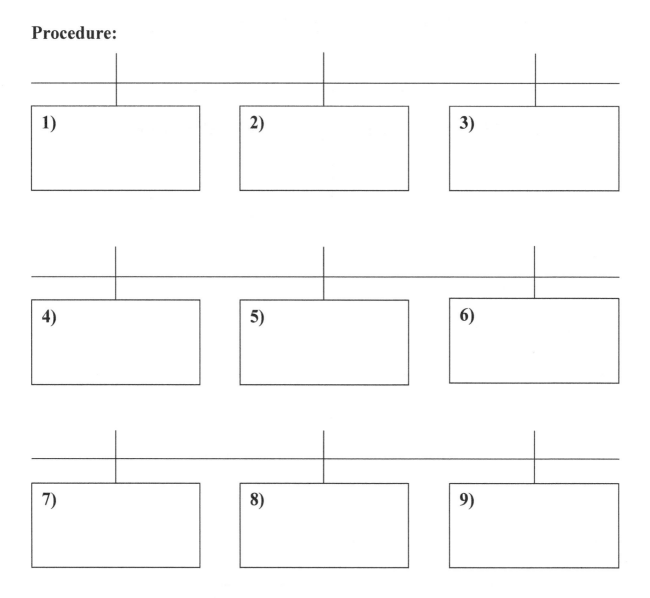

1)

2)

3)

4)

5)

6)

7)

8)

9)

## CCSS.ELA-Literacy.RST.6-8.4

Determine the meaning of symbols, key terms, and other domain-specific words and phrases as they are used in a specific scientific or technical context relevant to *grades 6–8 texts and topics.*\*

## Explanation

This standard asks students to establish meanings for symbols, words, and phrases in a scientific/technical text. With this graphic organizer, students are able to write the symbol, word, or phrase in the left column and relate its meaning in the right column.

| Word/ Phrase/Symbol | Meaning |
|---|---|
| | |
| | |
| | |
| | |

## CCSS.ELA-Literacy.RST.6-8.5

Analyze the structure an author uses to organize a text, including how the major sections contribute to the whole and to an understanding of the topic.*

## Explanation

This standard asks students to examine how the structure of a scientific/technical text influences its holistic and topical development. With this graphic organizer, students are able to identify the text structure at the top, identify the major text sections in the first table, and explain how those major sections contribute to the whole and to an understanding of the topic in the second table.

**Text Structure (Choose One: Chronological/Sequence, Cause/Effect, Problem/Solution, Compare/Contrast, Description, or Directions):**

| Major Section 1 | Major Section 2 | Major Section 3 | Major Section 4 |
|---|---|---|---|
|  |  |  |  |

| Contribution to Whole | Contribution to Understanding the Topic |
|---|---|
|  |  |

# CCSS.ELA-Literacy.RST.6-8.6

Analyze the author's purpose in providing an explanation, describing a procedure, or discussing an experiment in a text.*

## Explanation

This standard asks students to examine a scientific/technical author's purpose in a text. With this graphic organizer, students are able to identify the author's purpose in the left column and analyze it in the right column.

| **Author's Purpose** (Choose One: Providing an Explanation, Describing a Procedure, or Discussing an Experiment) | **Purpose Analysis** |
|---|---|
| | |
| | |
| | |

## <u>CCSS.ELA-Literacy.RST.6-8.7</u>

Integrate quantitative or technical information expressed in words in a text with a version of that information expressed visually (e.g., in a flowchart, diagram, model, graph, or table).*

## <u>Explanation</u>

This standard asks students to combine various scientific/technical material. With this graphic organizer, students are able to identify worded and visual information in the top two boxes and integrate that information in the bottom box.

| <u>Words</u> | <u>Visual</u> |
|---|---|
| a. <br><br> b. <br><br> c. <br><br> d. | |

## <u>Integration</u>

# CCSS.ELA-Literacy.RST.6-8.8

Distinguish among facts, reasoned judgment based on research findings, and speculation in a text.*

## Explanation

This standard asks students to differentiate between authentic information, a rational decision based on evidence, and an assumption in a scientific/technical text. With this graphic organizer, students are able to identify facts in the first column, reasoned judgment based on research findings in the second column, and speculation in the third column. Space is provided below to explain their distinctions.

| Fact | Reasoned Judgment Based on Research Findings | Speculation |
|------|---------------------------------------------|-------------|
|      |                                             |             |

## Distinction Explanation:

_____

_____

_____

_____

_____

_____

_____

## CCSS.ELA-Literacy.RST.6-8.9

Compare and contrast the information gained from experiments, simulations, video, or multimedia sources with that gained from reading a text on the same topic.*

## Explanation

This standard asks students to note the similarities and differences of different representations of the same scientific/technical topic. With this graphic organizer, students are able to write the topic/source names at the top, identify differences in the non-intersecting parts of the circles and identify similarities in the intersection of the two circles.

**Topic:**

**Experiments/Simulations/Video/Multimedia:**      **Text:**

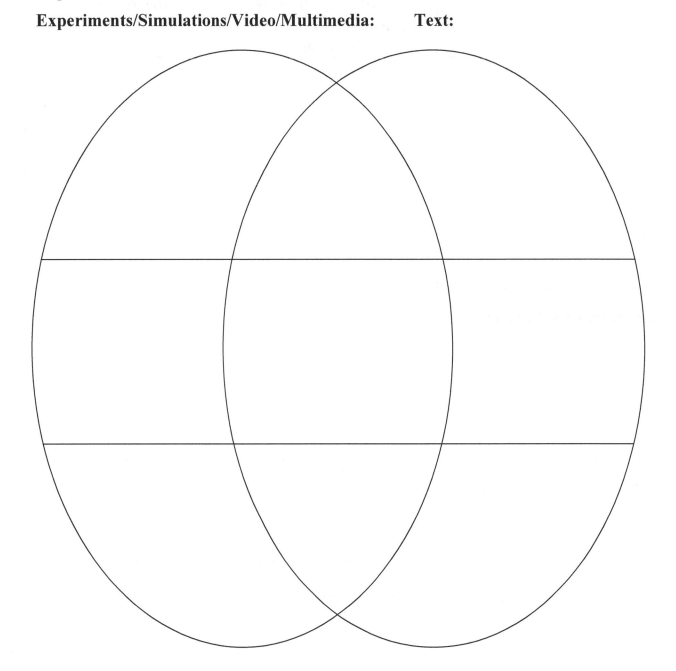

## CCSS.ELA-Literacy.RST.6-8.10

By the end of grade 8, read and comprehend science/technical texts in the grades 6–8 text complexity band independently and proficiently.*

## Explanation

This standard asks students to read scientific/technical texts that are grade-level appropriate. No table or graphic organizer is applicable

# Section 4

9th–10th Grade

Graphic Organizers

# CHAPTER 18

# 9th–10th Grade
# Reading Informational Text

# CCSS.ELA-Literacy.RI.9-10.1

Cite strong and thorough textual evidence to support analysis of what the text says explicitly as well as inferences drawn from the text.*

## Explanation

This standard asks students to indicate significant proof of explicit and inferential meaning within an informational text. With this graphic organizer, students are able to analyze for explicit and inferential meaning in the top row, relate evidence for those individual meanings in the middle row, and explain strength and thoroughness of the evidence in the bottom row.

| Explicit Meaning | |
|---|---|
| Textual Evidence | |
| Why is the textual evidence strong/thorough? | |

| Inferential Meaning | |
|---|---|
| Textual Evidence | |
| Why is the textual evidence strong/thorough? | |

# CCSS.ELA-Literacy.RI.9-10.2

Determine a central idea of a text and analyze its development over the course of the text, including how it emerges and is shaped and refined by specific details; provide an objective summary of the text.*

# Explanation

This standard asks students to establish the essential idea and examine how it progresses, originates, is influenced, and is clarified through details within an informational text, then summarize. With this graphic organizer, students are able to express the central idea in the big box at the top and relate details and how they develop, emerge, shape, and refine the central idea in the small boxes below. Space is provided for a summary as well.

## Central Idea

| Detail 1 | Detail 2 | Detail 3 |
|---|---|---|
| Emergence, Shaping, Refinement | Emergence, Shaping, Refinement | Emergence, Shaping, Refinement |

**Summary:**

_____

_____

_____

_____

_____

_____

_____

_____

## CCSS.ELA-Literacy.RI.9-10.3

Analyze how the author unfolds an analysis or series of ideas or events, including the order in which the points are made, how they are introduced and developed, and the connections that are drawn between them.*

## Explanation

This standard asks students to examine an informational text's sequence, presentation, and conceptual interactions. With this graphic organizer, students are able to write the idea/event at the top, relate the order in which points are made in the first column, explain how points are introduced and developed in the second column, and identify connections between points in the third column.

### Idea/Event:

| Order of Points Made | How Points Are Introduced and Developed | Connections Between Points |
|---|---|---|
| | | |

# CCSS.ELA-Literacy.RI.9-10.4

Determine the meaning of words and phrases as they are used in a text, including figurative, connotative, and technical meanings; analyze the cumulative impact of specific literary device on meaning and tone (e.g., how the language of a court opinion differs from that of a newspaper). *

## Explanation

This standard asks students to establish different meanings for words and phrases in an informational text and determine the relation of a literary device to meaning and tone. With this graphic organizer, students are able to use the left table to write a word or phrase in the first column and describe its various definitions in the second column. Students are able to use the right table to write the literary device used in the first column and analyze its impact on meaning and tone in the second column.

| Word/ Phrase | Definition |
|---|---|
| | Figurative- |
| | Connotative- |
| | Technical- |

| Literary Device | Impact Analysis |
|---|---|
| How the Language of Court Differs from That of a Newspaper- | Meaning- |
| | Tone- |

## CCSS.ELA-Literacy.RI.9-10.5

Analyze in detail how an author's ideas or claims are developed and refined by particular sentences, paragraphs, or larger portions of a text (e.g., a section or chapter).*

## Explanation

This standard asks students to examine how an author's thought is advanced through specific parts of an informational text. With this graphic organizer, students are able to write the author's idea or claim in the left column, identify particular sentences, paragraphs, or larger portions that refine and develop it in the middle column, and explain how those sentences, paragraphs, or larger portions of a text refine and develop the idea or claim in the right column.

| Idea/ Claim | Sentences/Paragraphs/ Chapter/Section | How Idea/Claim is Refined and Developed |
|---|---|---|
|  |  |  |
|  |  |  |

# CCSS.ELA-Literacy.RI.9-10.6

Determine an author's point of view or purpose in a text and analyze how an author uses rhetoric to advance that point of view or purpose.*

## Explanation

This standard asks students to establish an author's point of view or purpose in an informational text and examine how he/she uses language to demonstrate it. With this graphic organizer, students are able to write the author's point of view or purpose in the left column, identify rhetoric used to advance it in the middle column, and explain how the rhetoric advances point of view or purpose in the right column.

| Author's Point of View/Purpose | Rhetoric Used to Advance Point of View/Purpose | How Rhetoric Advances Point of View/Purpose |
|---|---|---|
| | | |

## CCSS.ELA-Literacy.RI.9-10.7

Analyze various accounts of a subject told in different mediums (e.g., a person's life story in both print and multimedia), determining which details are emphasized in each account.*

## Explanation

This standard asks students to examine how different media forms accentuate the same topic and establish which elements are focused on. With this graphic organizer, students are able to write the subject at the top and mediums in the 1st row and relate which details are emphasized within each medium in the corresponding columns.

## Subject:

| Medium #1:<br>Details Emphasized | Medium #2:<br>Details Emphasized | Medium #3:<br>Details Emphasized |
|---|---|---|
| | | |

## CCSS.ELA-Literacy.RI.9-10.8

Delineate and evaluate the argument and specific claims in a text, assessing whether the reasoning is valid and the evidence is relevant and sufficient; identify false statements and fallacious reasoning.*

## Explanation

This standard asks students to outline and assess an informational author's argument or claim in terms of reasons and evidence and recognize what is untrue and illogical. With this graphic organizer, students are able to write the author's argument or claim in the top box, delineate reasons and evidence in the first column, evaluate validity of reasons and relevancy/sufficiency of evidence in the second column, and identify fallacious reasons and false statements in the third column.

### Argument/Claim

| Delineation | Evaluation | Identification |
|---|---|---|
| Reasons- | Validity of Reasons- | Fallacious Reasoning- |
| Evidence- | Relevancy/Sufficiency of Evidence- | False Statements- |

# CCSS.ELA-Literacy.RI.9-10.9

Analyze seminal U.S. documents of historical and literary significance (e.g., Washington's Farewell Address, the Gettysburg Address, Roosevelt's Four Freedoms speech, King's "Letter from Birmingham Jail"), including how they address related themes and concepts.*

# Explanation

This standard asks students to examine how various historical and literary documents deal with similar topics and ideas. With this graphic organizer, students are able to write the documents' names in the 1st row and a related theme/concept in the first column and analyze how each document addresses that related theme/concept in the corresponding columns.

| Related Theme/ Concept | Document #1: How Related Theme/Concept is Addressed | Document #2: How Related Theme/Concept is Addressed | Document #3: How Related Theme/Concept is Addressed |
|---|---|---|---|
|  |  |  |  |

# CCSS.ELA-Literacy.RI.9-10.10

By the end of grade 9, read and comprehend literacy nonfiction in the grades 9-10 text complexity band proficiently, with scaffolding as needed at the high end of the range.*

By the end of grade 10, read and comprehend literary nonfiction at the high end of the grades 9-10 text complexity band independently and proficiently.*

# Explanation

This standard asks students to read nonfiction texts that are grade-level appropriate. No table or graphic organizer is applicable.

CHAPTER 19

# 9th–10th Grade
# Reading Literature Text

# CCSS.ELA-Literacy.RL.9-10.1

Cite strong and thorough textual evidence to support analysis of what the text says explicitly as well as inferences drawn from the text.*

## Explanation

This standard asks students to indicate significant proof of explicit and inferential meaning within a literature text. With this graphic organizer, students are able to analyze for explicit and inferential meaning in the top row, relate evidence for those individual meanings in the middle row, and explain strength and thoroughness of the evidence in the bottom row.

| | |
|---|---|
| **Explicit Meaning** | |
| **Textual Evidence** | |
| **Why is the textual evidence strong/thorough?** | |

| | |
|---|---|
| **Inferential Meaning** | |
| **Textual Evidence** | |
| **Why is the textual evidence strong/thorough?** | |

# CCSS.ELA-Literacy.RL.9-10.2

Determine a theme or central idea/theme of a text and analyze in detail its development over the course of the text, including how it emerges and is shaped and refined by specific details; provide an objective summary of the text.*

## Explanation

This standard asks students to establish the essential idea/theme of a literature text and how it progresses, originates, is influenced, and is clarified through details, then summarize. With this graphic organizer, students are able to express the central idea/theme in the big box at the top and relate how details develop, emerge, shape, and refine the central idea in the small boxes. Space is provided for a summary as well.

## Central Idea/Theme

| Detail 1 | Detail 2 | Detail 3 |
|---|---|---|
| Emergence, Shaping, Refinement | Emergence, Shaping, Refinement | Emergence, Shaping, Refinement |

## Summary:

_____

_____

_____

_____

_____

_____

_____

_____

# CCSS.ELA-Literacy.RL.9-10.3

Analyze how complex characters (e.g., those with multiple or conflicting motivations) develop over the course of a text, interact with other characters, and advance the plot or develop the theme.*

## Explanation

This standard asks students to examine how a story's characters evolve, connect to other characters, and move the story forward or progress a guiding idea. With this graphic organizer, students are able to write the character's name in the first column, relate how he/she develops in the second column, explain how he/she interacts in the third column, and describe how he/she advances the plot or develops the theme in the fourth column.

| Complex Character | Develops | Interacts | Advances Plot/ Develops Theme |
|---|---|---|---|
|  |  |  |  |

| Complex Character | Develops | Interacts | Advances Plot/ Develops Theme |
|---|---|---|---|
|  |  |  |  |

## CCSS.ELA-Literacy.RL.9-10.4

Determine the meaning of words and phrases as they are used in the text, including figurative and connotative meanings; analyze the cumulative impact of specific literary device on meaning and tone (e.g., how the language evokes a sense of time and place; how it sets a formal or informal tone).*

## Explanation

This standard asks students to establish different meanings for words and phrases in a literature text and determine the relation of a literary device on meaning and tone. With this graphic organizer, students are able to use the left table to write a word or phrase in the first column and describe its various definitions in the second column. Students are able to use the right table to write the literary device used in the first column and analyze its impact on meaning and tone in the second column.

| Word/ Phrase | Definition |
|---|---|
| | Figurative- |
| | Connotative- |

| Literary Device | Impact Analysis |
|---|---|
| How the Language Evokes a Sense of Time/Place- | Meaning- |
| How the Language Sets a Formal or Informal Tone- | Tone- |

## <u>CCSS.ELA-Literacy.RL.9-10.5</u>

Analyze how an author's choices concerning how to structure a text, order events within it (e.g., parallel plots), and manipulate time (e.g., pacing, flashbacks) create such effects as mystery, tension, or surprise.*

## <u>Explanation</u>

This standard asks students to determine how a literature text's elements produce certain effects. With this graphic organizer, students are able to analyze how structure creates mystery, tension, or surprise in the second column, how event order creates mystery, tension, or surprise in the third column, and how time manipulation creates mystery, tension, or surprise in the fourth column.

|  | Structure | Event Order | Time Manipulation |
|---|---|---|---|
| **Mystery** |  |  |  |
| **Tension** |  |  |  |
| **Surprise** |  |  |  |

# CCSS.ELA-Literacy.RL.9-10.6

Analyze a particular point of view or cultural experience reflected in a work of literature from outside the United States, drawing on a wide reading of world literature.*

## Explanation

This standard asks students to determine point of view or cultural experience in a multi-cultural literature text. With this graphic organizer, students are able to write the name of the work at the top, identify the point of view/ cultural experience in the left column, and relate how it is reflected through specific story episodes in the right column.

## Literary Work from Outside the United States:

| Point of View/Cultural Experience | Reflection |
|---|---|
| | **Episode-** |
| | **Episode-** |
| | **Episode-** |

## CCSS.ELA-Literacy.RL.9-10.7

Analyze the representation of a subject or a key scene in two different artistic mediums, including what is emphasized or absent in each treatment (e.g., Auden's "MusÃ©e des Beaux Arts" and Breughel's Landscape with the Fall of Icarus).*

## Explanation

This standard asks students to examine what is accentuated and missing from a scene/subject of literature that is represented in two different mediums. With this graphic organizer, students are able to write the names of the key scene/subject and mediums at the top, analyze what one medium emphasizes and deemphasizes in the first two columns and what the other medium emphasizes and deemphasizes in the second two columns.

**Subject/Key Scene:**
**Medium #1:**
**Medium #2:**

| Medium #1 Emphasis | Medium #1 Absence | Medium #2 Emphasis | Medium #2 Absence |
|---|---|---|---|
|  |  |  |  |

## CCSS.ELA-Literacy.RL.9-10.9

Analyze how an author draws on and transforms source material in a specific work (e.g., how Shakespeare treats a theme or topic from Ovid or the Bible or how a later author draws on a play by Shakespeare).*

## Explanation

This standard asks students to examine how an author uses a past literary work within his/her literary work. With this graphic organizer, students are able to write the past/current work and author at the top, analyze how the later author draws on a past source material in the left column, and relate how his/her work is transformed from past source material in the right column.

**Past Work/Author:**
**Later Work/Author:**

| How Later Work Draws On Past Work | How Later Work is Transformed from Past Work |
| --- | --- |
|  |  |

## <u>CCSS.ELA-Literacy.RL.9-10.10</u>

By the end of grade 9, read and comprehend literature, including stories, dramas, and poems, in the grades 9-10 text complexity band proficiently, with scaffolding as needed at the high end of the range.*

By the end of grade 10, read and comprehend literature, including stories, dramas, and poems, at the high end of the grades 9-10 text complexity band independently and proficiently.*

## <u>Explanation</u>

This standard asks students to read literature texts that are grade-level appropriate. No table or graphic organizer is applicable.

CHAPTER 20

# 9th–10th Grade Writing

# CCSS.ELA-Literacy.W.9-10.1

Write arguments to support claims in an analysis of substantive topics or texts, using valid reasoning and relevant and sufficient evidence.*

# CCSS.ELA-Literacy.W.9-10.1.a

Introduce precise claim(s), distinguish the claim(s) from alternate or opposing claims, and create an organization that establishes clear relationships among claim(s), counterclaims, reasons, and evidence.*

# CCSS.ELA-Literacy.W.9-10.1.b

Develop claim(s) and counterclaims fairly, supplying evidence for each while pointing out the strengths and limitations of both in a manner that anticipates the audience's knowledge level and concerns.*

# Explanation

This group of standards asks students to write to persuade an audience through the use of claim, reasons, and evidence, while distinguishing and supplying support for counter claims, and analyzing for strengths and limitations. With this graphic organizer, students are able to indicate the audience's knowledge/concern level at the top, brainstorm claim, alternate claim, and the distinction between them in the top table, and brainstorm reasons/evidence and analyze for strengths and limitations in the bottom table.

### Audience's Knowledge/Concern Level-Choose One: Low, Medium, High

| Claim | Counterclaim | Distinction between Claims |
|---|---|---|
|  |  |  |

| Support For Claim | Support For Counterclaim |
|---|---|
| Reasons- | Reasons- |
| Evidence- | Evidence- |
| Strengths- | Strengths- |
| Limitations- | Limitations- |

# CCSS.ELA-Literacy.W.9-10.1

Write arguments to support claims in an analysis of substantive topics or texts, using valid reasoning and relevant and sufficient evidence.*

# CCSS.ELA-Literacy.W.9-10.1.c

Use words, phrases, and clauses to link the major sections of the text, create cohesion, and clarify the relationships between claim(s) and reasons, between reasons and evidence, and between claim(s) and counterclaims.*

# Explanation

This standard asks students to use particular language to associate claim, counterclaim, reasons, and evidence within persuasive writing. With this graphic organizer, students are able to use the top table to write the claim in the left column, write reasons in the middle column, and brainstorm words, phrases, and/or clauses that link sections, create cohesion, and clarify the relationship among them in the right column. Students are able to use the middle table to write reasons in the left column, write evidence in the middle column, and brainstorm words, phrases, and/or clauses that link sections, create cohesion, and clarify the relationship among them in the right column. Students are able to use the bottom table to write a claim in the first column, write a counterclaim in the second column, and brainstorm words, phrases, and/or clauses that link sections, create cohesion, and clarify the relationship among them in the third column.

| Claim | Reasons | Words/Phrases/Clauses That Clarify |
|---|---|---|
| | 1 | |
| | 2 | |
| | 3 | |

| Reasons | Evidence | Words/Phrases/Clauses That Clarify |
|---|---|---|
| 1 | 1 | |
| 2 | 2 | |
| 3 | 3 | |

| Claim | Counterclaim | Words/Phrases/Clauses That Clarify |
|---|---|---|
| | | |

## CCSS.ELA-Literacy.W.9-10.1

Write arguments to support claims in an analysis of substantive topics or texts, using valid reasoning and relevant and sufficient evidence.*

## CCSS.ELA-Literacy.W.9-10.1.d

Establish and maintain a formal style and objective tone while attending to the norms and conventions of the discipline in which they are writing.*

## Explanation

This standard asks students to have a formal and objective writing style with accepted rules for persuasive writing. Because this standard leaves room for a teacher's interpretation, this example guide allows for modeling and guided practice so that students understand the difference between formal/objective and informal/biased writing styles.

## Informal/Biased Writing Style:

_____

_____

_____

_____

_____

_____

_____

## Formal/Objective Writing Style:

_____

_____

_____

_____

_____

_____

_____

## CCSS.ELA-Literacy.W.9-10.1

Write arguments to support claims in an analysis of substantive topics or texts, using valid reasoning and relevant and sufficient evidence.*

## CCSS.ELA-Literacy.W.9-10.1.e

Provide a concluding statement or section that follows from and supports the argument presented.*

## Explanation

This standard asks students to write a conclusion for persuasive writing. With this graphic organizer, students are able to write claim, reasons, and/or evidence in the top three boxes and, based on that, brainstorm a logical conclusion in the bottom box.

| Claim/Reason/ Evidence 1 | Claim/Reason/ Evidence 2 | Claim/Reason/ Evidence 3 |
| --- | --- | --- |
| | | |

**Conclusion**

## CCSS.ELA-Literacy.W.9-10.2

Write informative/explanatory texts to examine and convey complex ideas, concepts, and information clearly and accurately through the effective selection, organization, and analysis of content.*

## CCSS.ELA-Literacy.W.9-10.2.a

Introduce a topic; organize complex ideas, concepts, and information to make important connections and distinctions; include formatting (e.g., headings), graphics (e.g., figures, tables), and multimedia when useful to aiding comprehension.*

## Explanation

This standard asks students to utilize introduction, organization using connections and distinctions, formatting, and graphics/multimedia for informative/explanatory writing. With this graphic organizer, students are able to write the topic at the top, brainstorm an introduction in the first table, organization with connections/distinctions in the second table, formatting in the third table, and graphics/multimedia in the fourth table.

### Topic:

| Introduction | |
|---|---|
| - <br> - | - <br> - |

| Organization | | | |
|---|---|---|---|
| **Idea/Concept 1** | **Idea/Concept 2** | **Idea/Concept 3** | **Idea/Concept 4** |
| | | | |
| **Connections/ Distinctions** | **Connections/ Distinctions** | **Connections/ Distinctions** | **Connections/ Distinctions** |
| | | | |

| Formatting <br> (Headings) |
|---|
| |

| Graphics/Multimedia <br> (Charts, Tables) |
|---|
| |

## CCSS.ELA-Literacy.W.9-10.2

Write informative/explanatory texts to examine and convey complex ideas, concepts, and information clearly and accurately through the effective selection, organization, and analysis of content.*

## CCSS.ELA-Literacy.W.9-10.2.b

Develop the topic with well-chosen, relevant, and sufficient facts, extended definitions, concrete details, quotations, or other information and examples appropriate to the audience's knowledge of the topic.*

## Explanation

This standard asks students to have the micro elements of facts, definitions, details, quotations, and examples that are appropriate for their audience for informative/explanatory writing. With this graphic organizer, students are able to write the topic/the audience's knowledge level at the top and brainstorm these elements inside.

**Topic:**
**Audience's Knowledge Level:  Choose One-Low, Medium, High**

| Development |
| --- |
| **Well-Chosen/Relevant/Sufficient Facts-** |
| **Extended Definitions-** |
| **Concrete Details-** |
| **Quotations-** |
| **Other Information/Examples-** |

## CCSS.ELA-Literacy.W.9-10.2

Write informative/explanatory texts to examine and convey complex ideas, concepts, and information clearly and accurately through the effective selection, organization, and analysis of content.*

## CCSS.ELA-Literacy.W.9-10.2.c

Use appropriate and varied transitions to link the major sections of the text, create cohesion, and clarify the relationships among complex ideas and concepts.*

## Explanation

This standard asks students to use particular words to associate segments of informative/explanatory writing. With this graphic organizer, students are able to write major sections of the text in the left table and brainstorm transitions that link the major sections of the text, create cohesion, and clarify how they relate in the right boxes.

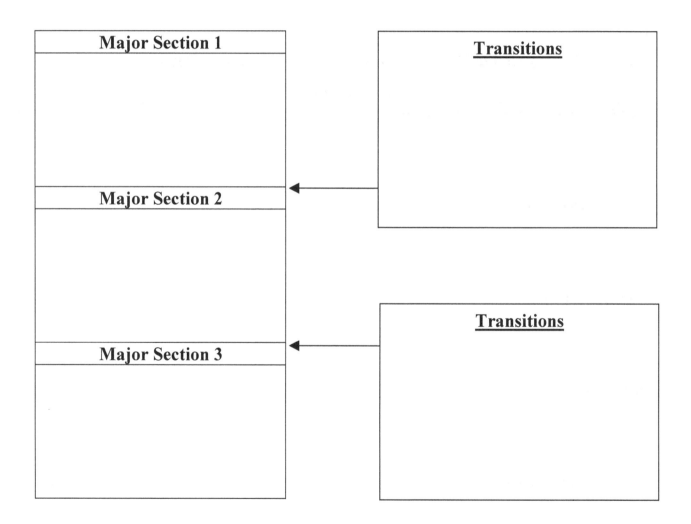

## CCSS.ELA-Literacy.W.9-10.2

Write informative/explanatory texts to examine and convey complex ideas, concepts, and information clearly and accurately through the effective selection, organization, and analysis of content.*

## CCSS.ELA-Literacy.W.9-10.2.d

Use precise language and domain-specific vocabulary to manage the complexity of the topic.*

## Explanation

This standard asks students to utilize certain subject matter words within informative/explanatory writing. With this graphic organizer, students are able to write the topic at the top and brainstorm precise domain-specific vocabulary that relates to the topic inside.

**Topic:**

| Precise/Domain-Specific Vocabulary |
|---|
| |

## CCSS.ELA-Literacy.W.9-10.2

Write informative/explanatory texts to examine and convey complex ideas, concepts, and information clearly and accurately through the effective selection, organization, and analysis of content.*

## CCSS.ELA-Literacy.W.9-10.2.e

Establish and maintain a formal style and objective tone while attending to the norms and conventions of the discipline in which they are writing.*

## Explanation

This standard asks students to have a formal and objective writing style with accepted rules for informative/explanatory writing. Because this standard leaves room for a teacher's interpretation, this example guide allows for modeling and guided practice so that students understand the difference between formal/objective and informal/biased writing styles.

## Informal Writing/Biased Style:

_____

_____

_____

_____

_____

_____

_____

## Formal/Objective Writing Style:

_____

_____

_____

_____

_____

_____

_____

## CCSS.ELA-Literacy.W.9-10.2

Write informative/explanatory texts to examine and convey complex ideas, concepts, and information clearly and accurately through the effective selection, organization, and analysis of content.*

## CCSS.ELA-Literacy.W.9-10.2.f

Provide a concluding statement or section that follows from and supports the information or explanation presented (e.g., articulating implications or the significance of the topic).*

## Explanation

This standard asks students to write a conclusion for informative/explanatory writing. With this graphic organizer, students are able to write concepts or ideas presented in the top three boxes and, based on that, brainstorm a logical conclusion in the bottom box.

| Concept/Idea 1 | Concept/Idea 2 | Concept/Idea 3 |
| --- | --- | --- |
| | | |

**Conclusion**

# CCSS.ELA-Literacy.W.9-10.3

Write narratives to develop real or imagined experiences or events using effective technique, well-chosen details, and well-structured event sequences.*

# CCSS.ELA-Literacy.W.9-10.3.a

Engage and orient the reader by setting out a problem, situation, or observation, establishing one or multiple point(s) of view, and introducing a narrator and/or characters; create a smooth progression of experiences or events.*

# CCSS.ELA-Literacy.W.9-10.3.b

Use narrative techniques, such as dialogue, pacing, description, reflection, and multiple plot lines, to develop experiences, events, and/or characters.*

# CCSS.ELA-Literacy.W.9-10.3.d

Use precise words and phrases, telling details, and sensory language to convey a vivid picture of the experiences, events, setting, and/or characters.*

# Explanation

This group of standards asks students to have the macro elements of context, point of view, characters, and event sequence and micro elements of dialogue, pacing, description, reflection, multiple plot lines, precise language, telling details, and sensory language that develop experiences, events, setting, and/or characters in narrative writing. With this graphic organizer, students are able to brainstorm these elements, making sure they relate.

## Establish

| Problem/Situation/Observation:<br><br>Characters/Narrator:<br><br>Point(s) of View: |
| --- |

## Event Sequence

| Event 1 | Narrative Technique (Choose):<br>Dialogue, Pacing, Reflection, Description, or Multiple Plot Lines | To Develop (Choose): |
| --- | --- | --- |
|  | precise words and phrases, telling details, and sensory language: | Events, Experiences, Characters, or Setting |

*Continued on next page

| Event 2 | Narrative Technique (Choose):<br>Dialogue, Pacing, Reflection, Description, or Multiple Plot Lines | To Develop (Choose): |
|---------|---|---|
| | precise words and phrases, telling details, and sensory language: | Events, Experiences, Characters, or Setting |

| Event 3 | Narrative Technique (Choose):<br>Dialogue, Pacing, Reflection, Description, or Multiple Plot Lines | To Develop (Choose): |
|---------|---|---|
| | precise words and phrases, telling details, and sensory language: | Events, Experiences, Characters, or Setting |

| Event 4 | Narrative Technique (Choose):<br>Dialogue, Pacing, Reflection, Description, or Multiple Plot Lines | To Develop (Choose): |
|---------|---|---|
| | precise words and phrases, telling details, and sensory language: | Events, Experiences, Characters, or Setting |

| Event 5 | Narrative Technique (Choose):<br>Dialogue, Pacing, Reflection, Description, or Multiple Plot Lines | To Develop (Choose): |
|---------|---|---|
| | precise words and phrases, telling details, and sensory language: | Events, Experiences, Characters, or Setting |

## CCSS.ELA-Literacy.W.9-10.3

Write narratives to develop real or imagined experiences or events using effective technique, well-chosen details, and well-structured event sequences.*

## CCSS.ELA-Literacy.W.9-10.3.c

Use a variety of techniques to sequence events so that they build on one another to create a coherent whole.*

## Explanation

This standard asks students to use particular language to express time progression within narrative writing. With this graphic organizer, students are able to write events in the left table and brainstorm techniques to sequence events so that they build on one another to create a coherent whole in the right boxes.

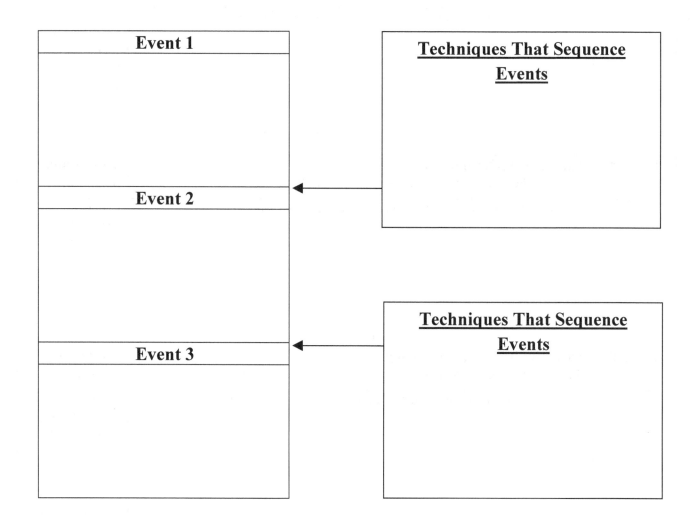

## CCSS.ELA-Literacy.W.9-10.3

Write narratives to develop real or imagined experiences or events using effective technique, well-chosen details, and well-structured event sequences.*

## CCSS.ELA-Literacy.W.9-10.3.e

Provide a conclusion that follows from and reflects on what is experienced, observed, or resolved over the course of the narrative.*

## Explanation

This standard asks students to write a conclusion for narrative writing. With this graphic organizer, students are able to write experiences, resolutions, or observations of the narrative in the top three boxes and, based on that, brainstorm a logical conclusion in the bottom box.

| Observation/ Resolution/ Experience 1 | Observation/ Resolution/ Experience 2 | Observation/ Resolution/ Experience 3 |
|---|---|---|
| | | |

**Conclusion**

# CCSS.ELA-Literacy.W.9-10.4

Produce clear and coherent writing in which the development, organization, and style are appropriate to task, purpose, and audience. (Grade-specific expectations for writing types are defined in standards 1–3 above.)*

## Explanation

This standard asks students to have clear/coherent writing for persuasive, informative/explanatory, and narrative texts. Because this standard leaves room for a teacher's interpretation, this example guide allows for modeling and guided practice so that students understand the difference between unclear/incoherent and clear/coherent writing styles.

## Unclear/Incoherent Writing Style:

_____

_____

_____

_____

_____

_____

_____

## Clear/Coherent Writing Style:

_____

_____

_____

_____

_____

_____

_____

# CCSS.ELA-Literacy.W.9-10.5

Develop and strengthen writing as needed by planning, revising, editing, rewriting, or trying a new approach, focusing on addressing what is most significant for a specific purpose and audience. (Editing for conventions should demonstrate command of Language standards 1-3 up to and including grades 9–10 here.)*

# Explanation

This standard asks students to use the writing process for persuasive, informative/explanatory, and narrative texts. No table or graphic organizer is applicable.

## **CCSS.ELA-Literacy.W.9-10.6**

Use technology, including the Internet, to produce, publish, and update individual or shared writing products, taking advantage of technology's capacity to link to other information and to display information flexibly and dynamically.*

## **Explanation**

This standard asks students to use technology for persuasive, informative/explanatory, and narrative texts. No table or graphic organizer is applicable.

## CCSS.ELA-Literacy.W.9-10.7

Conduct short as well as more sustained research projects to answer a question (including a self-generated question) or solve a problem; narrow or broaden the inquiry when appropriate; synthesize multiple sources on the subject, demonstrating understanding of the subject under investigation.*

## Explanation

This standard asks students to find information from various sources for research writing, change the focus if necessary, and summarize research information. With this graphic organizer, students are able to propose a question/problem at the top, identify information from various sources in the top boxes, make sure it is related to their research question at the top, and synthesize information found for the demonstration of understanding in the big box at the bottom. Space is provided to consider narrowing or broadening the inquiry.

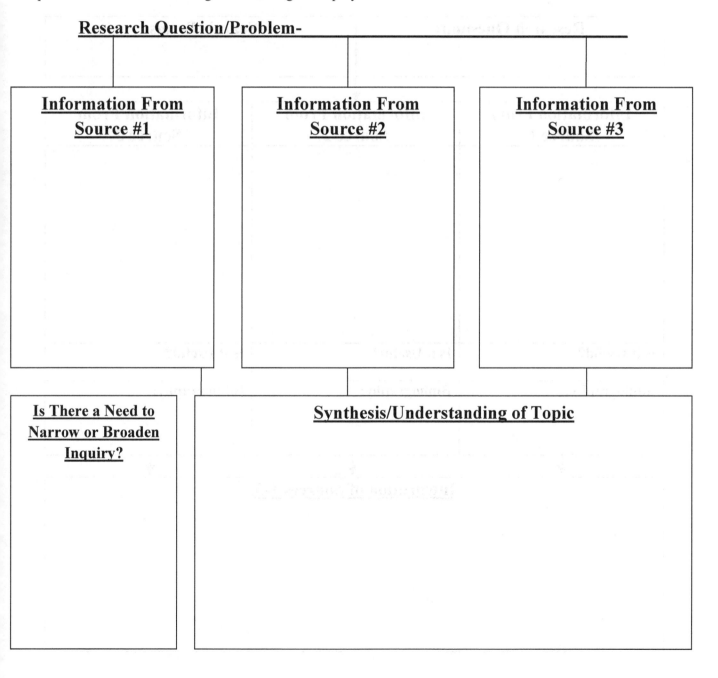

## <u>CCSS.ELA-Literacy.W.9-10.8</u>

Gather relevant information from multiple authoritative print and digital sources, using advanced searches effectively; assess the usefulness of each source in answering the research question; integrate information into the text selectively to maintain the flow of ideas, avoiding plagiarism and following a standard format for citation.*

## <u>Explanation</u>

This standard asks students to find pertinent information, utilize searches, evaluate the value of information, synthesize the information in a cohesive manner without plagiarism, and cite sources. With this graphic organizer, students are able to propose the research question and brainstorm search terms in the first table, gather information/assess its usefulness/include bibliography in the second table, and integrate information in the third table.

| <u>Research Question:</u> | <u>Search Terms:</u> |
|---|---|
| | |

| Information From Source 1 | Information From Source 2 | Information From Source 3 |
|---|---|---|
| | | |
| Is it Useful? | Is it Useful? | Is it Useful? |
| Bibliography: | Bibliography: | Bibliography: |

| <u>Integration of Sources 1-3</u> |
|---|
| |

## CCSS.ELA-Literacy.W.9-10.9

Draw evidence from literary or informational texts to support analysis, reflection, and research.*

## CCSS.ELA-Literacy.W.9-10.9.a

Apply *grades 9–10 Reading standards* to literature (e.g., "Analyze how an author draws on and transforms source material in a specific work [e.g., how Shakespeare treats a theme or topic from Ovid or the Bible or how a later author draws on a play by Shakespeare]").*

## CCSS.ELA-Literacy.W.9-10.9.b

Apply *grades 9–10 Reading standards* to literary nonfiction (e.g., "Delineate and evaluate the argument and specific claims in a text, assessing whether the reasoning is valid and the evidence is relevant and sufficient; identify false statements and fallacious reasoning").*

## Explanation

This group of standards asks students to write for the purpose of expressing the reading standards. With the first example guide, students are able to link a literature reading standard at the top to related analysis, reflection, and research below it. With the second example guide, students are able to link a literary nonfiction reading standard at the top to related analysis, reflection, and research below it.

**Literature Standard:**_____

**Analysis/Reflection/Research:**

_____

_____

_____

_____

_____

**Nonfiction Standard:**_____

**Analysis/Reflection/Research:**

_____

_____

_____

_____

_____

## <u>CCSS.ELA-Literacy.W.9-10.10</u>

Write routinely over extended time frames (time for research, reflection, and revision) and shorter time frames (a single sitting or a day or two) for a range of tasks, purposes, and audiences.*

## <u>Explanation</u>

This standard asks students to write short and long pieces of writing. No table or graphic organizer is applicable.

CHAPTER 21

# 9th–10th Grade
# Speaking/Listening

## CCSS.ELA-Literacy.SL.9-10.1

Initiate and participate effectively in a range of collaborative discussions (one-on-one, in groups, and teacher-led) with diverse partners on grades 9–10 topics, texts, and issues, building on others' ideas and expressing their own clearly and persuasively.*

## CCSS.ELA-Literacy.SL.9-10.1.a

Come to discussions prepared, having read and researched material under study; explicitly draw on that preparation by referring to evidence from texts and other research on the topic or issue to stimulate a thoughtful, well-reasoned exchange of ideas.*

## Explanation

This standard asks students to be ready with topical evidence for class discussions. With this graphic organizer, students are able write the topic/issue at the top and prepare using an outline, a graphic organizer, or both.

### Topic/Issue of Discussion:

| Evidence From Reading/Studying: | Evidence From Reading/Studying: |
|---|---|
| I.<br>A.<br>B.<br>C.<br><br>II.<br>A.<br>B.<br>C.<br><br>III.<br>A.<br>B.<br>C.<br><br>IV.<br>A.<br>B.<br>C.<br><br>V.<br>A.<br>B.<br>C. | |

## CCSS.ELA-Literacy.SL.9-10.1

Initiate and participate effectively in a range of collaborative discussions (one-on-one, in groups, and teacher-led) with diverse partners on grades 9–10 topics, texts, and issues, building on others' ideas and expressing their own clearly and persuasively.*

## CCSS.ELA-Literacy.SL.9-10.1.b

Work with peers to set rules for collegial discussions and decision-making (e.g., informal consensus, taking votes on key issues, presentation of alternate views), clear goals and deadlines, and individual roles as needed.*

## Explanation

This standard asks students to participate with classmates in setting class discussion norms. With this graphic organizer, students are able to write the topic/issue at the top, propose rules, goals, deadlines, and roles in the middle column, and work with peers on a consensus for those elements in the right column.

### Topic/Issue of Discussion:

|  | Student | Work With Peers |
|---|---|---|
| **Rules** |  |  |
| **Goals** |  |  |
| **Deadlines** |  |  |
| **Individual Roles** |  |  |

# CCSS.ELA-Literacy.SL.9-10.1

Initiate and participate effectively in a range of collaborative discussions (one-on-one, in groups, and teacher-led) with diverse partners on grades 9–10 topics, texts, and issues, building on others' ideas and expressing their own clearly and persuasively.*

# CCSS.ELA-Literacy.SL.9-10.1.c

Propel conversations by posing and responding to questions that relate the current discussion to broader themes or larger ideas; actively incorporate others into the discussion; and clarify, verify, or challenge ideas and conclusions.*

# Explanation

This standard asks students to participate in class discussion with questions and comments that relate to more general issues, involve classmates, and explain or confront issues. With this graphic organizer, students are able to write the topic/issue at the top and pose questions and responses that relate to boarder themes or larger ideas in the second row, actively incorporate others in the third row, and clarify/verify/challenge ideas and conclusions in the fourth row.

## Topic/Issue of Discussion:

|  | Questions | Responses |
|---|---|---|
| **Related to Broader Themes or Larger Ideas** |  |  |
| **Actively Incorporate Others** |  |  |
| **Clarify, Verify, or Challenge Ideas and Conclusions** |  |  |

## CCSS.ELA-Literacy.SL.9-10.1

Initiate and participate effectively in a range of collaborative discussions (one-on-one, in groups, and teacher-led) with diverse partners on grades 9–10 topics, texts, and issues, building on others' ideas and expressing their own clearly and persuasively.*

## CCSS.ELA-Literacy.SL.9-10.1.d

Respond thoughtfully to diverse perspectives, summarize points of agreement and disagreement, and, when warranted, qualify or justify their own views and understanding and make new connection in light of the evidence and reasoning presented.*

## Explanation

This standard asks students to reply to various perspectives in class discussions, review where positions agree and disagree, defend their perspective, and make new associations. With this graphic organizer, students are able to write the topic/issue, their view, and others' views at the top, record points of agreement and disagreement in the first two columns, qualify/justify their view in the third column, and make new connections in the fourth column.

### Topic/Issue of Discussion:

Your View:

_____

_____

Others' Views:

_____

_____

_____

| Points of Agreement | Points of Disagreement | Qualification/ Justification of Your View | New Connections |
|---|---|---|---|
| | | | |

## CCSS.ELA-Literacy.SL.9-10.2

Integrate multiple sources of information presented in diverse media or formats (e.g., visually, quantitatively, orally) evaluating the credibility and accuracy of each source.*

## Explanation

This standard asks students to combine various informational material and evaluate each source's reliability and precision. With this graphic organizer, students are able to identify various information and evaluate credibility/accuracy in the top three boxes and integrate that information in the box at the bottom.

| **Visual** | **Quantitative** | **Oral** |
|---|---|---|
| a.<br><br>b.<br><br><br>Is it credible/accurate? | a.<br><br>b.<br><br><br>Is it credible/accurate? | a.<br><br>b.<br><br><br>Is it credible/accurate? |

**Integration of Sources**

## CCSS.ELA-Literacy.SL.9-10.3

Evaluate a speaker's point of view, reasoning, and use of evidence and rhetoric, identifying any fallacious reasoning or exaggerated or distorted evidence.*

## Explanation

This standard asks students to assess a speaker's point of view in terms of explanations, proof, and word choice, then recognize what was misleading. With this graphic organizer, students are able to write/evaluate the speaker's point of view in the top box, evaluate the reasons, evidence, and rhetoric in the left column, and identify fallaciousness reasoning and exaggerated/distorted evidence in the right column.

| Point of View | Evaluation of Point of View |
|---|---|
| | |

| Evaluation | Identification |
|---|---|
| Reasons- | Fallacious Reasons- |
| Evidence- | Exaggerated/Distorted Evidence- |
| Rhetoric- | |

## CCSS.ELA-Literacy.SL.9-10.4

Present information, findings, and supporting evidence clearly, concisely, and logically such that listeners can follow the line of reasoning and the organization, development, substance, and style are appropriate to purpose, audience, and task.*

## Explanation

This standard asks students to present findings in terms of connected reasons and evidence. With this graphic organizer, students are able to identify findings in the top box and organize/develop the substance of the presentation through reasons/evidence in the bottom box.

**Findings**

|  |
|  |

**Organization/Development/Substance**

| Line of Reasoning | Supporting Evidence |
|---|---|
| Reason 1- | Evidence 1- |
| Reason 2- | Evidence 2- |
| Reason 3- | Evidence 3- |
| Reason 4- | Evidence 4- |

# CCSS.ELA-Literacy.SL.9-10.5

Make strategic use of digital media (e.g., textual, graphical, audio, visual, and interactive elements) in presentations to enhance understanding of findings, reasoning, and evidence and to add interest.*

## Explanation

This standard asks students to incorporate purposeful digital media in class speeches. With this graphic organizer, students are able to brainstorm what they intend to present in the left column, relate what digital media could be utilized in the middle column, and explain how the media enhances understanding and adds interest in the right column.

| Presentation Information (Main Ideas) | Possible Digital Media Components (Textual, Graphical, Audio, Visual, and Interactive) | How the Digital Media Component Enhances Understanding/Adds Interest |
| --- | --- | --- |
|  |  |  |
|  |  |  |
|  |  |  |

## CCSS.ELA-Literacy.SL.9-10.6

Adapt speech to a variety of contexts and tasks, demonstrating command of formal English when indicated or appropriate. (See grades 9–10 Language standards 1 and 3 here for specific expectations.)*

## Explanation

This standard asks students to speak within a range of grade-level situations. No table or graphic organizer is applicable.

# CHAPTER 22

# 9th–10th Grade Language

## CCSS.ELA-Literacy.L.9-10.1

Demonstrate command of the conventions of standard English grammar and usage when writing or speaking.*

## CCSS.ELA-Literacy.L.9-10.1.a

Use parallel structure.*

## Explanation

This standard asks students to utilize parallel structure in the construction of sentences. With this example guide, students are given space to discern the difference between parallel and non-parallel grammatical structures.

**Non-parallel Structure:**

_____

**Parallel Structure:**

_____

**Non-parallel Structure:**

_____

**Parallel Structure:**

_____

**Non-parallel Structure:**

_____

**Parallel Structure:**

_____

**Non-parallel Structure:**

_____

**Parallel Structure:**

_____

## CCSS.ELA-Literacy.L.9-10.1

Demonstrate command of the conventions of standard English grammar and usage when writing or speaking.*

## CCSS.ELA-Literacy.L.9-10.1.b

Use various types of phrases (noun, verb, adjectival, adverbial, participial, prepositional, absolute) and clauses (independent, dependent; noun, relative, adverbial) to convey specific meanings and add variety and interest to writing or presentations.*

## Explanation

This standard asks students to utilize different phrases and clauses. With this example guide, students are given space to discern the differences between them.

**Noun Phrase:** _____ .

**Verb Phrase:** _____ .

**Adjectival Phrase:** _____ .

**Adverbial Phrase:** _____ .

**Participial Phrase:** _____ .

**Prepositional Phrase:** _____ .

**Absolute Phrase:** _____ .

**Independent Clause:** _____ .

**Dependent Clause:** _____ .

**Noun Clause:** _____ .

**Relative Clause:** _____ .

**Adverbial Clause:** _____ .

## CCSS.ELA-Literacy.L.9-10.2

Demonstrate command of the conventions of standard English capitalization, punctuation, and spelling when writing.*

## CCSS.ELA-Literacy.L.9-10.2.a

Use a semicolon (and perhaps a conjunctive adverb) to link two or more closely related independent clauses.*

## Explanation

This standard asks students to utilize a semicolon and conjunctive adverb to join two associated sentences. With this example guide, students are given space to construct these types of sentences.

_____;

_____.

_____;

_____.

_____;

_____.

_____;

_____.

_____;

_____.

_____;

_____.

## CCSS.ELA-Literacy.L.9-10.2

Demonstrate command of the conventions of standard English capitalization, punctuation, and spelling when writing.*

## CCSS.ELA-Literacy.L.9-10.2.b

Use a colon to introduce a list or quotation.*

## Explanation

This standard asks students to utilize a colon to initiate a list or quotation. With this example guide, students are given space to construct these types of sentences.

## List:

_____:

_____,_____, _____and _____.

## Quotation:

_____: " _____

_____."

## List:

_____:

_____,_____, _____and _____.

## Quotation:

_____: " _____

_____."

## CCSS.ELA-Literacy.L.9-10.2

Demonstrate command of the conventions of standard English capitalization, punctuation, and spelling when writing.*

## CCSS.ELA-Literacy.L.9-10.2.c

Spell correctly.*

## Explanation

This standard asks students to spell words precisely. No table or graphic organizer is applicable.

## <u>CCSS.ELA-Literacy.L.9-10.3</u>

Apply knowledge of language to understand how language functions in different contexts, to make effective choices for meaning or style, and to comprehend more fully when reading or listening.*

## <u>CCSS.ELA-Literacy.L.9-10.3.a</u>

Write and edit work so that it conforms to the guidelines in a style manual (e.g., *MLA Handbook*, Turabian's *Manual for Writers*) appropriate for the discipline and writing type.*

## <u>Explanation</u>

This standard asks students to follow established rules when writing and editing. No table or graphic organizer is applicable.

## CCSS.ELA-Literacy.L.9-10.4

Determine or clarify the meaning of unknown and multiple-meaning words and phrases based on *grades 9–10 reading and content*, choosing flexibly from a range of strategies.*

## CCSS.ELA-Literacy.L.9-10.4.a

Use context (e.g., the overall meaning of a sentence, paragraph, or text; a word's position or function in a sentence) as a clue to the meaning of a word or phrase.*

## Explanation

This standard asks students to utilize context for word definition clues. With this graphic organizer, students are able to write the unknown word or phrase in the left column, relate given clues to its meaning in the middle column, and make an educated guess about its definition in the right column.

| Unknown Word/Phrase | Possible Clue Words/ Overall Meaning/ Position or Function | Possible Meaning of Unknown Word/Phrase |
|---|---|---|
| | | |
| | | |
| | | |
| | | |
| | | |
| | | |
| | | |

## CCSS.ELA-Literacy.L.9-10.4

Determine or clarify the meaning of unknown and multiple-meaning words and phrases based on *grades 9–10 reading and content*, choosing flexibly from a range of strategies.*

## CCSS.ELA-Literacy.L.9-10.4.b

Identify and correctly use patterns of word changes that indicate different meanings or parts of speech (e.g., *analyze, analysis, analytical; advocate, advocacy*).*

## Explanation

This standard asks students to recognize and utilize common word modifications that specify various definitions or parts of speech. With this graphic organizer, students are able to write patterns of words in the left column, each word's different meaning in the middle column, each word's part of speech in the right column, and use the words correctly in a sentence in the space provided below the table.

| Words | Meaning | Part of Speech |
|---|---|---|
|  |  |  |
|  |  |  |
|  |  |  |

_____.

_____.

_____.

| Words | Meaning | Part of Speech |
|---|---|---|
|  |  |  |
|  |  |  |
|  |  |  |

_____.

_____.

_____.

## CCSS.ELA-Literacy.L.9-10.4

Determine or clarify the meaning of unknown and multiple-meaning words and phrases based on *grades 9–10 reading and content*, choosing flexibly from a range of strategies.*

## CCSS.ELA-Literacy.L.9-10.4.c

Consult general and specialized reference materials (e.g., dictionaries, glossaries, thesauruses), both print and digital, to find the pronunciation of a word or determine or clarify its precise meaning, its part of speech, or its etymology.*

## Explanation

This standard asks students to utilize reference resources for unknown words. With this graphic organizer, students are able to write the unknown word in the left column and relate the meaning, part of speech, etymology, and/or pronunciation in the right column.

| Unknown Word | Reference Material-Meaning/Part of Speech/Pronunciation/Etymology |
|---|---|
|  |  |
|  |  |
|  |  |
|  |  |
|  |  |
|  |  |
|  |  |
|  |  |

## CCSS.ELA-Literacy.L.9-10.4

Determine or clarify the meaning of unknown and multiple-meaning words and phrases based on *grades 9–10 reading and content*, choosing flexibly from a range of strategies.*

## CCSS.ELA-Literacy.L.9-10.4.d

Verify the preliminary determination of the meaning of a word or phrase (e.g., by checking the inferred meaning in context or in a dictionary).*

## Explanation

This standard asks students to utilize context and dictionaries for word definition confirmation. With this graphic organizer, students are able to write the unknown word or phrase in the left column, relate its preliminary meaning in the middle column, and verify the definition in the right column.

| Word/Phrase | Preliminary Determination of Meaning | Inferred Meaning in Context/Dictionary |
|---|---|---|
|  |  |  |
|  |  |  |
|  |  |  |
|  |  |  |
|  |  |  |
|  |  |  |
|  |  |  |
|  |  |  |
|  |  |  |
|  |  |  |
|  |  |  |
|  |  |  |
|  |  |  |

## CCSS.ELA-Literacy.L.9-10.5

Demonstrate understanding of figurative language, word relationships, and nuances in word meanings.*

## CCSS.ELA-Literacy.L.9-10.5.a

Interpret figures of speech (e.g., euphemism, oxymoron) in context and analyze their role in the text.*

## Explanation

This standard asks students to explain figures of speech and determine their function in a text. With this graphic organizer, students are able to write the figure of speech in the first row, interpret it in the second row, and analyze the figure of speech's role in the text in the third row.

| | | |
|---|---|---|
| **Figure of Speech** (Euphemism, Oxymoron) | | |
| **Interpretation** | | |
| **Analysis of Role in Text** | | |

## CCSS.ELA-Literacy.L.9-10.5

Demonstrate understanding of figurative language, word relationships, and nuances in word meanings.*

## CCSS.ELA-Literacy.L.9-10.5.b

Analyze nuances in the meaning of words with similar denotations.*

## Explanation

This standard asks students to determine the subtle definitional differences of related words. With this graphic organizer, students are able to write words with similar denotations in the top row and determine their nuanced meanings in the bottom row.

| Words with Similar Denotations | | | |
|---|---|---|---|
| **Nuanced Meaning** | | | |

| Words with Similar Denotations | | | |
|---|---|---|---|
| **Nuanced Meaning** | | | |

## CCSS.ELA-Literacy.L.9-10.6

Acquire and use accurately general academic and domain-specific words and phrases, sufficient for reading, writing, speaking, and listening at the college and career readiness level; demonstrate independence in gathering vocabulary knowledge when considering a word or phrase important to comprehension or expression.*

## Explanation

This standard asks students to use vocabulary that is grade-level appropriate and collect vocabulary information. For the former, no table or graphic organizer is applicable, and the latter is addressed in CCSS.ELA-Literacy.L.9-10.4.

CHAPTER 23

# 9th–10th Grade
# History/Social Studies

# CCSS.ELA-Literacy.RH.9-10.1

Cite specific textual evidence to support analysis of primary and secondary sources, attending to such features as the date and origin of the information.*

## Explanation

This standard asks students to indicate proof of examination of primary and secondary sources, with a focus on date and origin. With this graphic organizer, students are able to identify primary and secondary sources in the first row, analyze in the second row, relate textual evidence in the third row, and document date and origin in the fourth row.

|  | **Primary Source:** | **Secondary Source:** |
|---|---|---|
| **Analysis** |  |  |
| **Textual Evidence** |  |  |
| **Date/Origin** |  |  |

## CCSS.ELA-Literacy.RH.9-10.2

Determine the central ideas or information of a primary or secondary source; provide an accurate summary of how key events or ideas develop over the course of the text.*

## Explanation

This standard asks students to decide the essential ideas of a primary or secondary source, then summarize important events and ideas and how they develop. With this graphic organizer, students are able to write the source at the top, express the central ideas/information in the big box and document how key events or ideas develop over the course of the text in the small boxes. Space is provided for a summary as well.

**Source:**

### Central Ideas/Information

|  |
|  |

| Detail 1 | Detail 2 | Detail 3 |

| Detail 4 | Detail 5 | Detail 6 |

**Summary:**

_____

_____

_____

_____

_____

_____

## CCSS.ELA-Literacy.RH.9-10.3

Analyze in detail a series of events described in a text; determine whether earlier events caused later ones or simply preceded them.*

## Explanation

This standard asks students to chronicle historical or social events and decide if initial events caused subsequent ones. With this graphic organizer, students are able to document a series of events in a timeline format and determine whether earlier events caused later ones or simply preceded them in the space below.

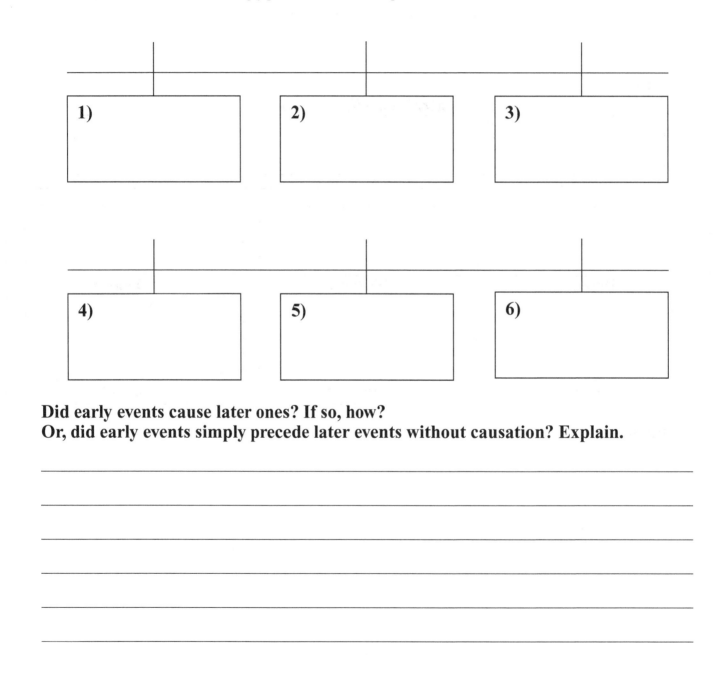

**Did early events cause later ones? If so, how?**
**Or, did early events simply precede later events without causation? Explain.**

_____

_____

_____

_____

_____

## CCSS.ELA-Literacy.RH.9-10.4

Determine the meaning of words and phrases as they are used in a text, including vocabulary describing political, social, or economic aspects of history/social science.*

## Explanation

This standard asks students to establish the meaning of words and phrases in a text that relate to political, social, or economic facets of history/social science. With this graphic organizer, students are able to write the word or phrase in the left column, identify the aspect it is related to in the middle column, and determine the word's or phrase's meaning in the right column.

| Word/ Phrase | Related To (Choose: Political, Social, or Economic Aspect) | Meaning |
|---|---|---|
|  |  |  |
|  |  |  |
|  |  |  |

# CCSS.ELA-Literacy.RH.9-10.5

Analyze how a text uses structure to emphasize key points or advance an explanation or analysis.*

## Explanation

This standard asks students to examine how a historical/social text's structure is utilized to highlight important details or progress a description/examination. With this graphic organizer, students are able to identify the text structure in the left column and relate how it is used to emphasize key points or advance an explanation/analysis in the right column.

| Structure of Text (Choose One: Chronological/Sequence, Cause/Effect, Problem/Solution, Compare/Contrast, Description, Directions) | How the Text Uses Structure to Emphasize Key Points/Advance an Explanation or Analysis |
|---|---|
| | |
| | |

# CCSS.ELA-Literacy.RH.9-10.6

Compare the point of view of two or more authors for how they treat the same or similar topics, including which details they include and emphasize in their respective accounts.*

## Explanation

This standard asks students to document the similar points of view of two historical/social authors who write on the same issue. With this graphic organizer, students are able to write the topic and author names at the top of the first table, then determine which details each author includes and emphasizes in the first table. Based on that, students are able to establish the authors' points of view in the second table and compare the authors' points of view in the third table.

**Topic:**

**Author 1:**                                      **Author 2:**

| Author 1-Details Included/Emphasized | Author 2-Details Included/Emphasized |
|---|---|
|  |  |

| Author 1-Point of View: | Author 2-Point of View: |
|---|---|
|  |  |

| Comparison: |
|---|
|  |

# CCSS.ELA-Literacy.RH.9-10.7

Integrate quantitative or technical analysis (e.g., charts, research data) with qualitative analysis in print or digital text.*

## Explanation

This standard asks students to combine various historical/social material. With this graphic organizer, students are able to write the text name at the top, identify quantitative or technical analysis in the top-left box, identify qualitative analysis in the top-right box, and integrate that information in the bottom box.

**Text:**

| **Quantitative/Technical Analysis** | **Qualitative Analysis** |
|---|---|
| a. | a. |
| b. | b. |
| c. | c. |
| d. | d. |

**Integration**

## CCSS.ELA-Literacy.RH.9-10.8

Assess the extent to which the reasoning and evidence in a text support the author's claims.*

## Explanation

This standard asks students to evaluate a historical/social author's claims in terms of support from reasons and evidence. With this graphic organizer, students are able to write the author's claim in the top box, relate reasons and evidence for that claim in the left column, and assess the reasons and evidence in the right column.

### Claim

| Reasons/Evidence | Assessment |
|---|---|
| Reasons- | Extent That Reasons Support Claim- |
| Evidence- | Extent That Evidence Supports Claim- |

## CCSS.ELA-Literacy.RH.9-10.9

Compare and contrast treatments of the same topic in several primary and secondary sources.*

## Explanation

This standard asks students to note the similarities and differences of how different primary and secondary sources chronicle the same issue. With this graphic organizer, students are able to write the topic at the top and sources in the small boxes, identify the differences between sources in the non-intersecting segments of the circles, and identify the similarities in the intersecting segments of the circles.

**Topic:**

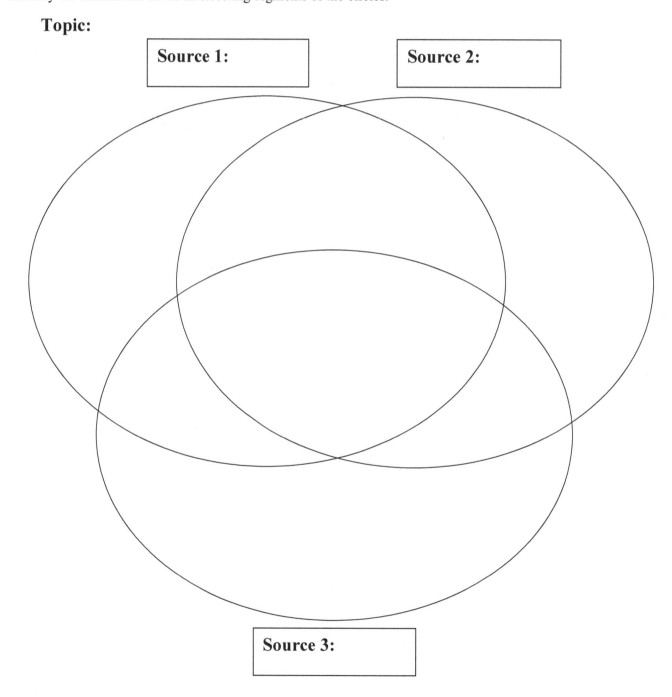

# CCSS.ELA-Literacy.RH.9-10.10

By the end of grade 10, read and comprehend history/social studies texts in the grades 9-10 text complexity band independently and proficiently.*

# Explanation

This standard asks students to read historical/social texts that are grade-level appropriate. No table or graphic organizer is applicable.

# CHAPTER 24

# 9th–10th Grade
# Science/Technical

## CCSS.ELA-Literacy.RST.9-10.1

Cite specific textual evidence to support analysis of science and technical texts, attending to the precise details of explanations or descriptions.*

## Explanation

This standard asks students to indicate proof of examination of scientific/technical texts, with a focus on accurate details. With this graphic organizer, students are able to analyze in the first row and relate textual evidence with precise details of explanations or descriptions in the second row.

| | |
|---|---|
| **Analysis** | |
| **Textual Evidence-Precise Details of Explanations/ Descriptions** | |

| | |
|---|---|
| **Analysis** | |
| **Textual Evidence-Precise Details of Explanations/ Descriptions** | |

## CCSS.ELA-Literacy.RST.9-10.2

Determine the central ideas or conclusions of a text; trace the text's explanation or depiction of a complex process, phenomenon, or concept; provide an accurate summary of the text.*

## Explanation

This standard asks students to establish the essential ideas/conclusions in a scientific/technical text, outline descriptions of a complicated procedure, theory, or principle, then summarize. With this graphic organizer, students are able to write the process, phenomenon, or concept at the top, express the central ideas/conclusions in the top boxes, and relate the explanation/depiction of the process, phenomenon, or concept in the bottom boxes. Space is provided for a summary as well.

**Process/Phenomenon/Concept:**

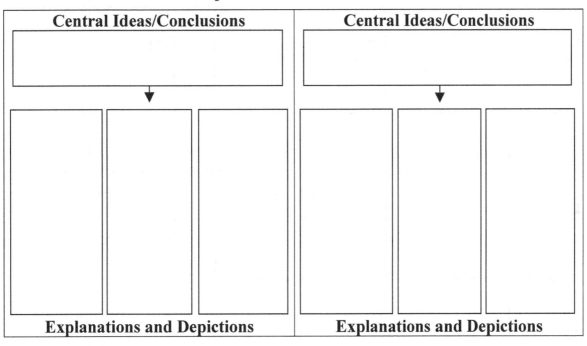

**Summary:**

_____

_____

_____

_____

_____

_____

_____

## CCSS.ELA-Literacy.RST.9-10.3

Follow precisely a complex multistep procedure when carrying out experiments, taking measurements, or performing technical tasks, attending to special cases or exceptions defined in the text.*

## Explanation

This standard asks students to adhere to a scientific/technical process with a focus on unique situations or exclusions. With this graphic organizer, students are able to write the name of the procedure at the top, document the procedure in a multistep format in the boxes, and attend to special cases or exemptions in the table at the bottom.

**Name of Procedure:**

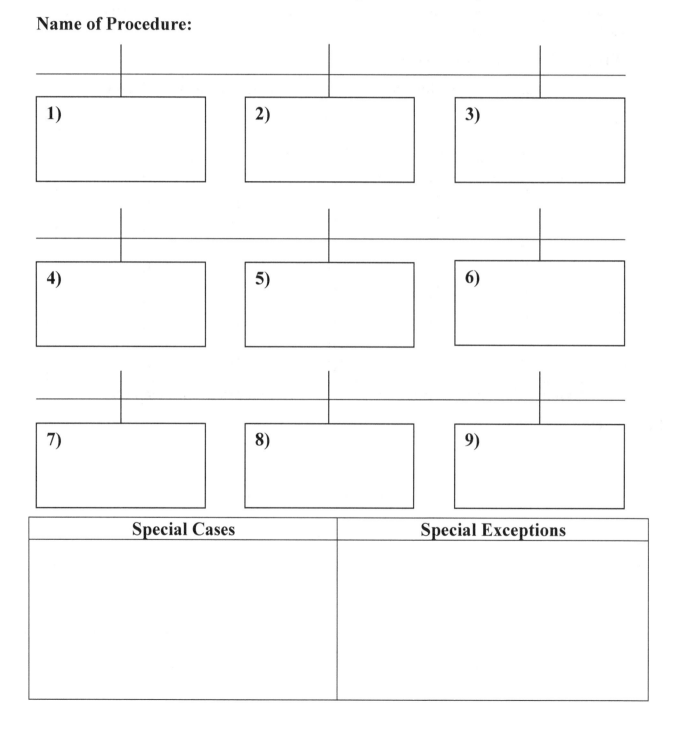

| Special Cases | Special Exceptions |
|---|---|
|  |  |

## CCSS.ELA-Literacy.RST.9-10.4

Determine the meaning of symbols, key terms, and other domain-specific words and phrases as they are used in a specific scientific or technical context relevant to *grades 9–10 texts and topics.**

## Explanation

This standard asks students to establish meanings for symbols, words, and phrases in a scientific/technical text. With this graphic organizer, students are able to write the symbol, word, or phrase in the left column and relate its meaning in the right column.

| Word/ Phrase/Symbol | Meaning |
|---|---|
|  |  |
|  |  |
|  |  |
|  |  |

## CCSS.ELA-Literacy.RST.9-10.5

Analyze the structure of the relationships among concepts in a text, including relationships among key terms (e.g.,*force, friction, reaction force, energy*).*

## Explanation

This standard asks students to examine the structural relationship among concepts in a scientific/technical text. With this graphic organizer, students are able to write the concept in the small boxes, use the non-intersecting segments of the circles to define each concept, and use the intersecting segments to analyze the structural relationships among concepts/terms.

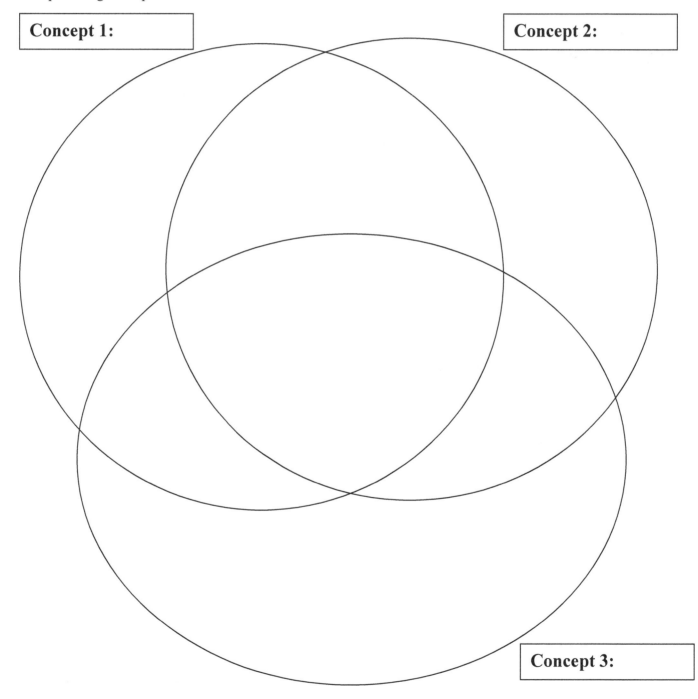

Concept 1:

Concept 2:

Concept 3:

## CCSS.ELA-Literacy.RST.9-10.6

Analyze the author's purpose in providing an explanation, describing a procedure, or discussing an experiment in a text, defining the question the author seeks to address.*

## Explanation

This standard asks students to examine an author's purpose and key question in a scientific/technical text. With this graphic organizer, students are able to write the question the author seeks to address at the top, identify the author's purpose in the left column, and analyze it in the right column.

### Question the Author Seeks to Address:

| Author's Purpose (Choose One: Providing an Explanation, Describing a Procedure, or Discussing an Experiment) | Purpose Analysis |
|---|---|
|  |  |
|  |  |

# CCSS.ELA-Literacy.RST.9-10.7

Translate quantitative or technical information expressed in words in a text into visual form (e.g., a table or chart) and translate information expressed visually or mathematically (e.g., in an equation) into words.*

# Explanation

This standard asks students to convert quantitative or technical material from words to visuals and visuals to words. With this graphic organizer, students are able to express words from a text in the top-left box and translate them into a visual in the top-right box. Then, students are able to express visual/mathematical information in the bottom-left box and translate it into words in the bottom-right box.

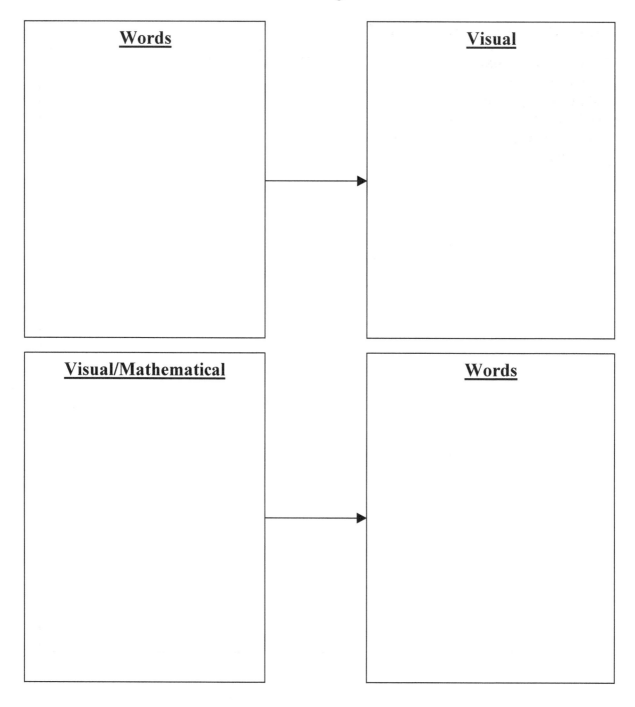

## CCSS.ELA-Literacy.RST.9-10.8

Assess the extent to which the reasoning and evidence in a text support the author's claim or a recommendation for solving a scientific or technical problem.*

## Explanation

This standard asks students to evaluate an author's claim or recommendation for a scientific/technical solution in terms of reasons and evidence. With this graphic organizer, students are able to write the author's claim or recommendation in the top box, relate reasons and evidence in the left column, and assess the reasons and evidence in the right column.

### Claim or Recommendation For Solving a Scientific/Technical Problem

| Reasons/Evidence | Assessment |
|---|---|
| Reasons- | Extent That Reasons Support Claim/Recommendation- |
| Evidence- | Extent That Evidence Supports Claim/Recommendation- |

## CCSS.ELA-Literacy.RST.9-10.9

Compare and contrast findings presented in a text to those from other sources (including their own experiments), noting when the findings support or contradict previous explanations or accounts.*

## Explanation

This standard asks students to document the similarities and differences of data in a scientific/technical text to those from other sources and note confirmation or opposition to past findings. With this graphic organizer, students are able to write the names of the text and other sources at the top, identify the findings' differences in the non-intersecting parts of the circles, identify the findings' similarities in the intersecting part of the circles, and note when the findings support or contradict previous explanations or accounts in the space at the bottom.

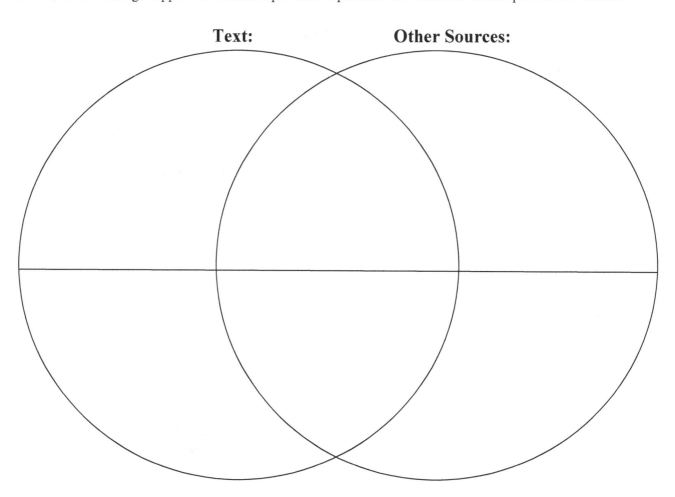

**Text:**                    **Other Sources:**

## Do the findings support or contradict previous explanations or accounts? Explain.

_____

_____

_____

_____

# CCSS.ELA-Literacy.RST.9-10.10

By the end of grade 10, read and comprehend science/technical texts in the grades 9–10 text complexity band independently and proficiently.*

## Explanation

This standard asks students to read scientific/technical texts that are grade-level appropriate. No table or graphic organizer is applicable.

# Section 5

11th–12th Grade

Graphic Organizers

# CHAPTER 25

# 11th–12th Grade
# Reading Informational Text

# CCSS.ELA-Literacy.RI.11-12.1

Cite strong and thorough textual evidence to support analysis of what the text says explicitly as well as inferences drawn from the text, including determining where the text leaves matters uncertain.*

## Explanation

This standard asks students to indicate powerful proof of explicit and inferential meaning for an informational text and indicate which issues remain vague. With this graphic organizer, students are able to analyze for explicit and inferential meaning in the first row, relate evidence for those individual meanings in the second row, examine strength and thoroughness of evidence in the third row, and explain matters left uncertain in the fourth row.

| | |
|---|---|
| **Explicit Meaning** | |
| **Textual Evidence** | |
| **Why is the textual evidence strong/thorough?** | |
| **Matters Left Uncertain** | |

| | |
|---|---|
| **Inferential Meaning** | |
| **Textual Evidence** | |
| **Why is the textual evidence strong/thorough?** | |
| **Matters Left Uncertain** | |

## CCSS.ELA-Literacy.RI.11-12.2

Determine two or more central ideas of a text and analyze their development over the course of the text, including how they interact and build on one another to provide a complex analysis; provide an objective summary of the text.*

## Explanation

This standard asks students to establish the essential themes/ideas and how they progress/interrelate within an informational text, then summarize. With this graphic organizer, students are able to express the central ideas in the second row, analyze their development in the third row, and analyze how they interact in the fourth row. Space is provided for a summary as well.

| | 1 | 2 | 3 |
|---|---|---|---|
| **Themes/ Ideas** | | | |
| **Development** | | | |
| **Interaction** | | | |

## Summary:

_____

_____

_____

_____

_____

## CCSS.ELA-Literacy.RI.11-12.3

Analyze a complex set of ideas or sequence of events and explain how specific individuals, ideas, or events interact and develop over the course of the text.*

## Explanation

This standard asks students to examine how an informational text's individuals, events, and ideas relate and develop. With this graphic organizer, students are able to use the intersecting segments of the circles to document how the different story elements interact with each other and the non-intersecting segments of the circles to document how the different story elements develop.

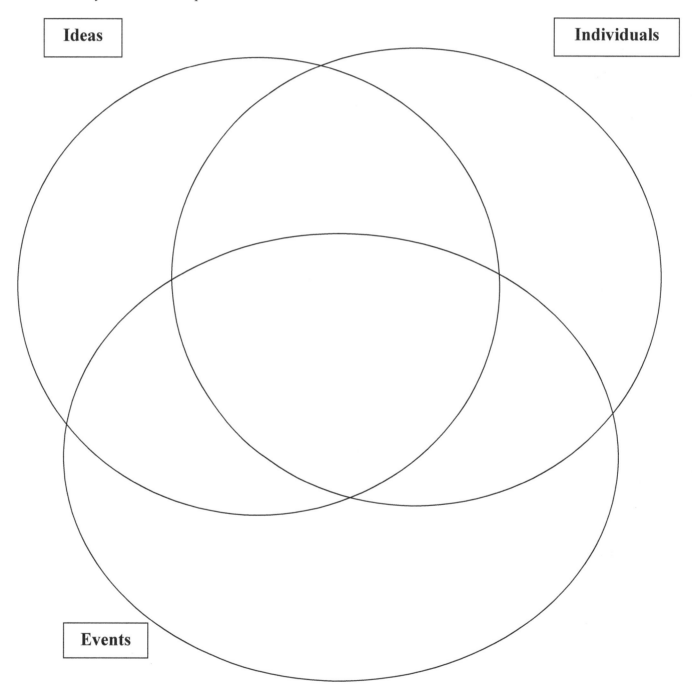

# CCSS.ELA-Literacy.RI.11-12.4

Determine the meaning of words and phrases as they are used in a text, including figurative, connotative, and technical meanings; analyze how an author uses and refines the meaning of a key term or terms over the course of a text (e.g., how Madison defines faction in Federalist No. 10).*

## Explanation

This standard asks students to establish different meanings for words and phrases in an informational text and examine how an important word is used and clarified throughout the text. With this graphic organizer, students are able to use the left table to write a word or phrase in the first column and describe its various definitions in the second column. Students are able to use the right table to write a key term in the first column and analyze how an author uses and refines the meaning of the key term over the course of a text in the second column.

| Word/ Phrase | Definition |
| --- | --- |
| | Figurative-<br><br><br><br>Connotative-<br><br><br><br>Technical- |

| Key Term | Use/Refinement Over the Course of a Text |
| --- | --- |
| | |

## <u>CCSS.ELA-Literacy.RI.11-12.5</u>

Analyze and evaluate the effectiveness of the structure an author uses in his or her exposition or argument, including whether the structure makes points clear, convincing, and engaging.*

## <u>Explanation</u>

This standard asks students to examine how an informational author structures a claim and to assess its effectiveness. With this graphic organizer, students are able to write the exposition or argument in the left column, relate the structure used in the middle column, and evaluate whether the structure makes points clear, convincing, and engaging in the right column.

| Exposition/ Argument | Analysis of Structure | Evaluation of Structure |
|---|---|---|
| | | **Clarity-** <br><br><br><br> **Conviction-** <br><br><br><br> **Engagement-** |

## CCSS.ELA-Literacy.RI.11-12.6

Determine an author's point of view or purpose in a text in which the rhetoric is particularly effective, analyzing how style and content contribute to the power, persuasiveness or beauty of the text.*

## Explanation

This standard asks students to establish an author's point of view or purpose in an informational text and language that is useful to it and examine how approach and words add to power, persuasiveness, or beauty of the text. With this graphic organizer, students are able to write the author's point of view or purpose in the left column, identify effective rhetoric in the middle column, and analyze how style and content contribute to power, persuasiveness, or beauty in the right column.

| Author's Point of View/ Purpose | Rhetoric Used Effectively | How Rhetorical Style and Content Contribute to: (Choose One: Power, Persuasiveness, or Beauty) |
|---|---|---|
|  |  |  |

## CCSS.ELA-Literacy.RI.11-12.7

Integrate and evaluate multiple sources of information presented in different media or formats (e.g., visually, quantitatively) as well as in words in order to address a question or solve a problem.*

## Explanation

This standard asks students to combine and assess various informational material to answer an inquiry or resolve a dilemma. With this graphic organizer, students are able to write the question/problem at the top, identify and evaluate various forms of information in the top three boxes, and integrate that information to address a question or solve a problem in the box at the bottom.

**Question/Problem-** _____

| **Visual** | **Quantitative** | **Verbal** |
|---|---|---|
| a.<br><br>b.<br><br>c.<br><br>Evaluation | a.<br><br>b.<br><br>c.<br><br>Evaluation | a.<br><br>b.<br><br>c.<br><br>Evaluation |

**Integration of Sources**

# CCSS.ELA-Literacy.RI.11-12.8

Delineate and evaluate the reasoning in seminal U.S. texts, including the application of constitutional principles and use of legal reasoning (e.g., in U.S. Supreme Court majority opinions and dissents) and the premises, purposes, and arguments in works of public advocacy (e.g., *The Federalist*, presidential addresses).*

## Explanation

This standard asks students to outline and assess particular concepts within various seminal U.S. texts/works of public advocacy. With this graphic organizer, students are able to use the top table to write the name of the seminal U.S. text at the top, delineate the application of constitutional principles and use of legal reasoning in the second column, and evaluate them in the third column. Students are able to use the bottom table to write the name of a work of public advocacy at the top, delineate the application of premises, purposes, and arguments in the second column, and evaluate them in the third column.

## Seminal U.S. Text:

|  | Delineation | Evaluation |
|---|---|---|
| **Application of Constitutional Principles** |  |  |
| **Use of Legal Reasoning** |  |  |

## Work of Public Advocacy:

|  | Delineation | Evaluation |
|---|---|---|
| **Premises** |  |  |
| **Purposes** |  |  |
| **Arguments** |  |  |

## CCSS.ELA-Literacy.RI.11-12.9

Analyze seventeenth-, eighteenth-, and nineteenth-century foundational U.S. documents of historical and literary significance (including The Declaration of Independence, the Preamble to the Constitution, the Bill of Rights, and Lincoln's Second Inaugural Address) for their themes, purposes, and rhetorical features.*

## Explanation

This standard asks students to examine important U.S. documents for their topics, functions, and use of language. With this graphic organizer, students are able to write the name of the document at the top, analyze themes in the second row, purposes in the third row, and rhetorical features in the fourth row.

### Seventeenth-, Eighteenth-, or Nineteenth- Century Foundational U.S. Document:

| | Analysis |
|---|---|
| **Themes** | |
| **Purposes** | |
| **Rhetorical Features** | |

## CCSS.ELA-Literacy.RI.11-12.10

By the end of grade 11, read and comprehend literary nonfiction in the grades 11–CCR text complexity band proficiently, with scaffolding as needed at the high end of the range.*

By the end of grade 12, read and comprehend literary nonfiction at the high end of the grades 11–CCR text complexity band independently and proficiently.*

## Explanation

This standard asks students to read nonfiction texts that are grade-level appropriate. No table or graphic organizer is applicable.

# CHAPTER 26

# 11th–12th Grade Reading Literature Text

# CCSS.ELA-Literacy.RL.11-12.1

Cite strong and thorough textual evidence to support analysis of what the text says explicitly as well as inferences drawn from the text, including determining where the text leaves matters uncertain.*

## Explanation

This standard asks students to indicate significant proof of explicit and inferential meaning for a literature text as well as indicate which issues remain vague. With this graphic organizer, students are able to analyze for explicit and inferential meaning in the first row, relate evidence for those individual meanings in the second row, explain strength and thoroughness of evidence in the third row, and describe matters left uncertain in the fourth row.

| | |
|---|---|
| **Explicit Meaning** | |
| **Textual Evidence** | |
| **Why is the textual evidence strong/thorough?** | |
| **Matters Left Uncertain** | |

| | |
|---|---|
| **Inferential Meaning** | |
| **Textual Evidence** | |
| **Why is the textual evidence strong/thorough?** | |
| **Matters Left Uncertain** | |

## CCSS.ELA-Literacy.RL.11-12.2

Determine two or more themes or central ideas of a text and analyze their development over the course of the text, including how they interact and build on one another to produce a complex account; provide an objective summary of the text.*

## Explanation

This standard asks students to establish the essential themes/ideas and how they progress and interrelate within a literature text, then summarize. With this graphic organizer, students are able to express the themes/central ideas in the second row, analyze their development in the third row, and analyze how they interact in the fourth row. Space is provided for a summary as well.

|  | 1 | 2 | 3 |
|---|---|---|---|
| **Themes/ Ideas** |  |  |  |
| **Development** |  |  |  |
| **Interaction** |  |  |  |

**Summary:**

_____

_____

_____

_____

_____

# CCSS.ELA-Literacy.RL.11-12.3

Analyze the impact of the author's choices regarding how to develop and relate elements of a story or drama (e.g., where a story is set, how the action is ordered, how the characters are introduced and developed).*

## Explanation

This standard asks students to examine how an author's choices influence his/her story's elements. With this graphic organizer, students are able to analyze the impact of the author's choices related to setting in the second column, how the action is ordered in the third column, and characters in the fourth column.

| | Setting | How Action is Ordered | Characters' Introduction/ Development |
|---|---|---|---|
| **Impact Analysis of Author's Choices** | | | |

# CCSS.ELA-Literacy.RL.11-12.4

Determine the meaning of words and phrases as they are used in the text, including figurative and connotative meanings; analyze the impact of specific literary device on meaning and tone, including words with multiple meanings or language that is particularly fresh, engaging, or beautiful. (Include Shakespeare as well as other authors.)*

## Explanation

This standard asks students to establish different meanings for words and phrases in a literature text and determine the relation of a specific literary device to meaning and tone. With this graphic organizer, students are able to use the left table to write a word or phrase in the first column and describe its various definitions in the second column. Students are able to use the right table to write the literary device used in the first column and analyze its impact on meaning and tone in the second column.

| Word/ Phrase | Definition |
|---|---|
| | Figurative- |
| | Connotative- |

| Literary Device | Impact Analysis |
|---|---|
| Multiple Meaning Words- | Meaning- |
| Fresh, Engaging, or Beautiful Language- | Tone- |

# CCSS.ELA-Literacy.RL.11-12.5

Analyze how an author's choices concerning how to structure specific parts of a text (e.g., the choice of where to begin or end a story, the choice to provide a comedic or tragic resolution) contribute to its overall structure and meaning as well as its aesthetic impact.*

## Explanation

This standard asks students to examine how an author's choice on text structure in a particular section fits into an overall story organization/implication and produces an artistic effect. With this graphic organizer, students are able to identify the author's choice in the first row and relate its contribution on the overall story structure/meaning in the second row and aesthetic impact in the third row.

| | Author's Choice on Structure (Choose One: Beginning or End/Comedic or Tragic Resolution) |
|---|---|
| **Contribution to Overall Structure/ Meaning** | |
| **Aesthetic Impact** | |

## CCSS.ELA-Literacy.RL.11-12.6

Analyze a case in which grasping a point of view requires distinguishing what is directly stated in a text from what is really meant (e.g., satire, sarcasm, irony, or understatement).*

## Explanation

This standard asks students to examine how the explicit and implicit meaning in a literature text relate to point of view. With this graphic organizer, students are able to write what is directly stated in the left column, explain what is really meant in the middle column, and relate the point of view in the right column.

| What is Directly Stated | What is Really Meant (Choose One to Explain: Satire, Sarcasm, Irony, or Understatement) | Point of View |
|---|---|---|
|  |  |  |

# CCSS.ELA-Literacy.RL.11-12.7

Analyze multiple interpretations of a story, drama, or poem (e.g., recorded or live production of a play or recorded novel or poetry), evaluating how each version interprets the source text. (Include at least one play by Shakespeare and one play by an American dramatist.)*

## Explanation

This standard asks students to examine and assess how a literary source text is interpreted in various productions. With this graphic organizer, students are able to write the text name at the top and version names in the first row, analyze how each version interprets the source text in the second row, and evaluate each version's interpretation in the third row.

### Story/Drama/Poem Source Text:

|  | Version #1: | Version #2: | Version #3: |
|---|---|---|---|
| **Interpretation Analysis** |  |  |  |
| **Evaluation** |  |  |  |

# CCSS.ELA-Literacy.RL.11-12.9

Demonstrate knowledge of eighteenth-, nineteenth- and early-twentieth-century foundational works of American literature, including how two or more texts from the same period treat similar themes or topics.*

## Explanation

This standard asks students to note the similarities of important works of American literature on the same guiding ideas or issues. With this graphic organizer, students are able to write the names of different texts in the first row and the similar theme/topic in the first column and analyze how the different texts treat the theme/topic in the corresponding columns.

| Theme/ Topic | Text 1: | Text 2: | Text 3: |
|---|---|---|---|
|  |  |  |  |

## CCSS.ELA-Literacy.RL.11-12.10

By the end of grade 11, read and comprehend literature, including stories, dramas, and poems, in the grades 11–CCR text complexity band proficiently, with scaffolding as needed at the high end of the range.*

By the end of grade 12, read and comprehend literature, including stories, dramas, and poems, at the high end of the grades 11–CCR text complexity band independently and proficiently.*

## Explanation

This standard asks students to read literature texts that are grade-level appropriate. No table or graphic organizer is applicable.

CHAPTER 27

# 11th–12th Grade
# Writing

# CCSS.ELA-Literacy.W.11-12.1

Write arguments to support claims in an analysis of substantive topics or texts, using valid reasoning and relevant and sufficient evidence.*

# CCSS.ELA-Literacy.W.11-12.1.a

Introduce precise, knowledgeable claim(s), establish the significance of the claim(s), distinguish the claim(s) from alternate or opposing claims, and create an organization that logically sequences claim(s), counterclaims, reasons, and evidence.*

# CCSS.ELA-Literacy.W.11-12.1.b

Develop claim(s) and counterclaims fairly and thoroughly, supplying the most relevant evidence for each while pointing out the strengths and limitations of both in a manner that anticipates the audience's knowledge level, concerns, values, and possible biases.*

## Explanation

This group of standards asks students to write to persuade an audience through the use of related claims/claim implications, reasons, and evidence, while distinguishing and supplying ample support for counter claims, and analyzing for strengths and limitations. With this graphic organizer, students are able to indicate the audience's knowledge, concern level, values, and bias at the top, brainstorm a significant claim, alternate claim, and the distinction between them in the top table, and brainstorm reasons/evidence and analyze for strengths and limitations in the bottom table.

### Audience's Values/Bias/Concerns/Knowledge: _____

| Claim | Counterclaim | Distinction between Claims |
|---|---|---|
|  |  |  |

| Support For Claim | Support For Counterclaim |
|---|---|
| Reasons- | Reasons- |
| Evidence- | Evidence- |
| Strengths- | Strengths- |
| Limitations- | Limitations- |

## CCSS.ELA-Literacy.W.11-12.1

Write arguments to support claims in an analysis of substantive topics or texts, using valid reasoning and relevant and sufficient evidence.*

## CCSS.ELA-Literacy.W.11-12.1.c

Use words, phrases, and clauses as well as varied syntax to link the major sections of the text, create cohesion, and clarify the relationships between claim(s) and reasons, between reasons and evidence, and between claim(s) and counterclaims.*

## Explanation

This standard asks students to use particular language to explain the association of claim, counterclaim, reasons, and evidence within persuasive writing. With this graphic organizer, students are able to use the top table to write the claim in the left column, write reasons in the middle column, and brainstorm words, phrases, clauses, and/ or varied syntax that link sections, create cohesion, and clarify the relationship among them in the right column. Students are able to use the middle table to write reasons in the left column, write evidence in the middle column, and brainstorm words, phrases, clauses, and/or varied syntax that that link sections, create cohesion, and clarify the relationship among them in the right column. Students are able to use the bottom table to write a claim in the first column, write a counterclaim in the second column, and brainstorm words, phrases, clauses, and/or varied syntax that link sections, create cohesion, and clarify the relationship among them in the third column.

| Claim | Reasons | | Words/Phrases/Clauses That Clarify/Varied Syntax |
|---|---|---|---|
| | 1 | | |
| | 2 | | |
| | 3 | | |

| Reasons | | Evidence | Words/Phrases/Clauses That Clarify/Varied Syntax |
|---|---|---|---|
| 1 | | 1 | |
| 2 | | 2 | |
| 3 | | 3 | |

| Claim | Counterclaim | Words/Phrases/Clauses That Clarify/Varied Syntax |
|---|---|---|
| | | |

## CCSS.ELA-Literacy.W.11-12.1

Write arguments to support claims in an analysis of substantive topics or texts, using valid reasoning and relevant and sufficient evidence.*

## CCSS.ELA-Literacy.W.11-12.1.d

Establish and maintain a formal style and objective tone while attending to the norms and conventions of the discipline in which they are writing.*

## Explanation

This standard asks students to have a formal and objective writing style with accepted rules for persuasive writing. Because this standard leaves room for a teacher's interpretation, this example guide allows for modeling and guided practice so that students understand the difference between formal/objective and informal/biased writing styles.

## Informal/Biased Writing Style:

_____

_____

_____

_____

_____

_____

_____

## Formal/Objective Writing Style:

_____

_____

_____

_____

_____

_____

_____

_____

# CCSS.ELA-Literacy.W.11-12.1

Write arguments to support claims in an analysis of substantive topics or texts, using valid reasoning and relevant and sufficient evidence.*

# CCSS.ELA-Literacy.W.11-12.1.e

Provide a concluding statement or section that follows from and supports the argument presented.*

# Explanation

This standard asks students to write a conclusion for persuasive writing. With this graphic organizer, students are able to write claim, reasons, and/or evidence in the top three boxes and, based on that, brainstorm a logical conclusion in the bottom box.

| **Claim/Reason/ Evidence 1** | **Claim/Reason/ Evidence 2** | **Claim/Reason/ Evidence 3** |
|---|---|---|
| | | |

**Conclusion**

## CCSS.ELA-Literacy.W.11-12.2

Write informative/explanatory texts to examine and convey complex ideas, concepts, and information clearly and accurately through the effective selection, organization, and analysis of content.*

## CCSS.ELA-Literacy.W.11-12.2.a

Introduce a topic; organize complex ideas, concepts, and information so that each new element builds on that which precedes it to create a unified whole; include formatting (e.g., headings), graphics (e.g., figures, tables), and multimedia when useful to aiding comprehension.*

## Explanation

This standard asks students to utilize introduction, organization by how each idea/concept builds off of the preceding one, formatting, and graphics/multimedia for informative/explanatory writing. With this graphic organizer, students are able to write the topic at the top and brainstorm an introduction in the first table, organization so that each new element builds on that which precedes it to create a unified whole in the second table, formatting in the third table, and graphics/multimedia in the fourth table.

### Topic:

| Introduction | |
|---|---|
| - | - |
| - | - |

| Organization | | | |
|---|---|---|---|
| **Idea/Concept 1** | **Idea/Concept 2** | **Idea/Concept 3** | **Idea/Concept 4** |
| | | | |
| | **How Idea/Concept 2 is built on Idea/Concept 1** | **How Idea/Concept 3 is built on Idea/Concept 2** | **How Idea/Concept 4 is built on Idea/Concept 3** |
| | | | |

| Formatting (Headings) |
|---|
| |

| Graphics/Multimedia (Charts, Tables) |
|---|
| |

# CCSS.ELA-Literacy.W.11-12.2

Write informative/explanatory texts to examine and convey complex ideas, concepts, and information clearly and accurately through the effective selection, organization, and analysis of content.*

# CCSS.ELA-Literacy.W.11-12.2.b

Develop the topic thoroughly by selecting the most significant and relevant facts, extended definitions, concrete details, quotations, or other information and examples appropriate to the audience's knowledge of the topic.*

# Explanation

This standard asks students to have the micro elements of facts, definitions, details, quotations, and examples that are appropriate for their audience for informative/explanatory writing. With this graphic organizer, students are able to write the topic/audience's knowledge level at the top and brainstorm these elements inside.

**Topic:**

**Audience's Knowledge Level:** Choose One-Low, Medium, High

| Development |
|---|
| **Significant/Relevant Facts-** |
| **Extended Definitions-** |
| **Concrete Details-** |
| **Quotations-** |
| **Other Information/Examples-** |

## CCSS.ELA-Literacy.W.11-12.2

Write informative/explanatory texts to examine and convey complex ideas, concepts, and information clearly and accurately through the effective selection, organization, and analysis of content.*

## CCSS.ELA-Literacy.W.11-12.2.c

Use appropriate and varied transitions and syntax to link the major sections of the text, create cohesion, and clarify the relationships among complex ideas and concepts.*

## Explanation

This standard asks students to use particular words to associate segments of informative/explanatory writing. With this graphic organizer, students are able to write major sections of the text in the left table and brainstorm transitions/syntax that link major sections of the text, create cohesion, and clarify how they relate in the right boxes.

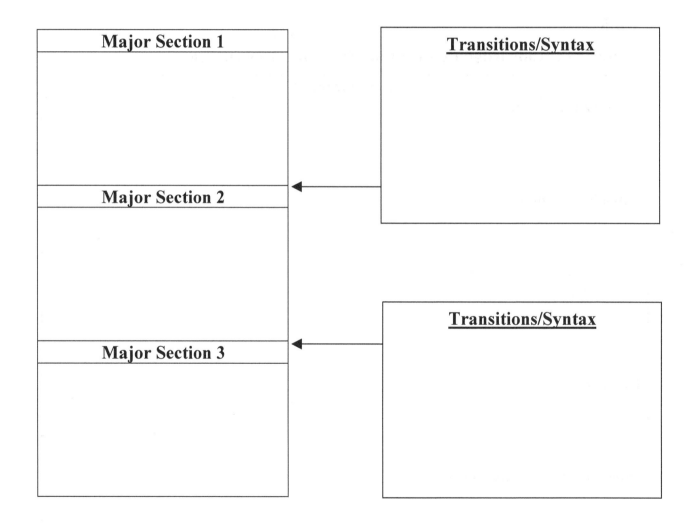

# CCSS.ELA-Literacy.W.11-12.2

Write informative/explanatory texts to examine and convey complex ideas, concepts, and information clearly and accurately through the effective selection, organization, and analysis of content.*

# CCSS.ELA-Literacy.W.11-12.2.d

Use precise language, domain-specific vocabulary, and techniques such as metaphor, simile, and analogy to manage the complexity of the topic.*

## Explanation

This standard asks students to utilize certain subject matter words and approaches to handle the intricacy of a topic explanation for informative/explanatory writing. With this graphic organizer, students are able to write the topic at the top and brainstorm precise domain-specific terms in the first table and techniques that manage the complexity of the topic in the second table.

### Topic:

| Precise/Domain-Specific Vocabulary |
| --- |
| |

| Techniques |
| --- |
| Simile- <br><br> Metaphor- <br><br> Analogy- |

## CCSS.ELA-Literacy.W.11-12.2

Write informative/explanatory texts to examine and convey complex ideas, concepts, and information clearly and accurately through the effective selection, organization, and analysis of content.*

## CCSS.ELA-Literacy.W.11-12.2.e

Establish and maintain a formal style and objective tone while attending to the norms and conventions of the discipline in which they are writing.*

## Explanation

This standard asks students to have a formal and objective writing style with accepted rules for informative/ explanatory writing. Because this standard leaves room for a teacher's interpretation, this example guide allows for modeling and guided practice so that students understand the difference between formal/objective and informal/ biased writing styles.

## Informal/Biased Writing Style:

_____

_____

_____

_____

_____

_____

_____

## Formal/Objective Writing Style:

_____

_____

_____

_____

_____

_____

_____

# CCSS.ELA-Literacy.W.11-12.2

Write informative/explanatory texts to examine and convey complex ideas, concepts, and information clearly and accurately through the effective selection, organization, and analysis of content.*

# CCSS.ELA-Literacy.W.11-12.2.f

Provide a concluding statement or section that follows from and supports the information or explanation presented (e.g., articulating implications or the significance of the topic).*

# Explanation

This standard asks students to write a conclusion for informative/explanatory writing. With this graphic organizer, students are able to write concepts or ideas presented in the top three boxes and, based on that, brainstorm a logical conclusion in the bottom box.

| Concept/Idea 1 | Concept/Idea 2 | Concept/Idea 3 |
|---|---|---|
| | | |

**Conclusion**

# CCSS.ELA-Literacy.W.11-12.3

Write narratives to develop real or imagined experiences or events using effective technique, well-chosen details, and well-structured event sequences.*

# CCSS.ELA-Literacy.W.11-12.3.a

Engage and orient the reader by setting out a problem, situation, or observation and its significance, establishing one or multiple point(s) of view, and introducing a narrator and/or characters; create a smooth progression of experiences or events.*

# CCSS.ELA-Literacy.W.11-12.3.b

Use narrative techniques, such as dialogue, pacing, description, reflection, and multiple plot lines, to develop experiences, events, and/or characters.*

# CCSS.ELA-Literacy.W.11-12.3.d

Use precise words and phrases, telling details, and sensory language to convey a vivid picture of the experiences, events, setting, and/or characters.*

# Explanation

This group of standards asks students to have the macro elements of context, point of view, characters, and event sequence and micro elements of dialogue, pacing, description, reflection, multiple plot lines, precise language, telling details, and sensory language that develop experiences, events, setting, and/or characters in narrative writing. With this graphic organizer, students are able to brainstorm these elements, making sure they relate.

## Establish

| Problem/Situation/Observation and Significance: |
|---|
| Characters/Narrator: |
| Point(s) of View: |

## Event Sequence

| Event 1 | **Narrative Technique (Choose):** Dialogue, Pacing, Reflection, Description, or Multiple Plot Lines | **To Develop (Choose):** |
|---|---|---|
| | precise words and phrases, telling details, and sensory language: | Events, Experiences, Characters, or Setting |

*Continued on next page

| Event 2 | **Narrative Technique (Choose):** Dialogue, Pacing, Reflection, Description, or Multiple Plot Lines | **To Develop (Choose):** |
|---|---|---|
| | precise words and phrases, telling details, and sensory language: | Events, Experiences, Characters, or Setting |

| Event 3 | **Narrative Technique (Choose):** Dialogue, Pacing, Reflection, Description, or Multiple Plot Lines | **To Develop (Choose):** |
|---|---|---|
| | precise words and phrases, telling details, and sensory language: | Events, Experiences, Characters, or Setting |

| Event 4 | **Narrative Technique (Choose):** Dialogue, Pacing, Reflection, Description, or Multiple Plot Lines | **To Develop (Choose):** |
|---|---|---|
| | precise words and phrases, telling details, and sensory language: | Events, Experiences, Characters, or Setting |

| Event 5 | **Narrative Technique (Choose):** Dialogue, Pacing, Reflection, Description, or Multiple Plot Lines | **To Develop (Choose):** |
|---|---|---|
| | precise words and phrases, telling details, and sensory language: | Events, Experiences, Characters, or Setting |

# CCSS.ELA-Literacy.W.11-12.3

Write narratives to develop real or imagined experiences or events using effective technique, well-chosen details, and well-structured event sequences.*

# CCSS.ELA-Literacy.W.11-12.3.c

Use a variety of techniques to sequence events so that they build on one another to create a coherent whole and build toward a particular tone and outcome (e.g., a sense of mystery, suspense, growth, or resolution).*

## Explanation

This standard asks students to use a mix of approaches to strategically relate and develop chronological progression in narrative writing. With this graphic organizer, students are able to indicate the desired outcome/tone at the top, identify event sequence in the second row, brainstorm sequencing techniques that produce the desired outcome/tone in the fourth row, and explain the desired effect of the technique in the sixth row.

**Tone/Outcome Being Built:** (Choose One: Mystery, Suspense, Growth or Resolution)

| Event 1 | Event 2 | Event 3 |
|---|---|---|
|  |  |  |
|  | Techniques that sequence event 1–2 | Techniques that sequence event 2–3 |
|  |  |  |
|  | Desired Effect | Desired Effect |
|  |  |  |

## CCSS.ELA-Literacy.W.11-12.3

Write narratives to develop real or imagined experiences or events using effective technique, well-chosen details, and well-structured event sequences.*

## CCSS.ELA-Literacy.W.11-12.3.e

Provide a conclusion that follows from and reflects on what is experienced, observed, or resolved over the course of the narrative.*

## Explanation

This standard asks students to write a conclusion for narrative writing. With this graphic organizer, students are able to write experiences, resolutions, or observations of the narrative in the top three boxes and, based on that, brainstorm a logical conclusion in the bottom box.

| Observation/ Resolution/ Experience 1 | Observation/ Resolution/ Experience 2 | Observation/ Resolution/ Experience 3 |
|---|---|---|

**Conclusion**

# CCSS.ELA-Literacy.W.11-12.4

Produce clear and coherent writing in which the development, organization, and style are appropriate to task, purpose, and audience. (Grade-specific expectations for writing types are defined in standards 1–3 above.)*

## Explanation

This standard asks students to have clear/coherent writing for persuasive, informative/explanatory, and narrative texts. Because this standard leaves room for a teacher's interpretation, this example guide allows for modeling and guided practice so that students understand the difference between unclear/incoherent and clear/coherent writing styles.

## Unclear/Incoherent Writing Style:

_____

_____

_____

_____

_____

_____

_____

## Clear/Coherent Writing Style:

_____

_____

_____

_____

_____

_____

_____

_____

## CCSS.ELA-Literacy.W.11-12.5

Develop and strengthen writing as needed by planning, revising, editing, rewriting, or trying a new approach, focusing on addressing what is most significant for a specific purpose and audience. (Editing for conventions should demonstrate command of Language standards 1–3 up to and including grades 11–12 here.)*

## Explanation

This standard asks students to use the writing process for persuasive, informative/explanatory, and narrative texts. No table or graphic organizer is applicable.

# CCSS.ELA-Literacy.W.11-12.6

Use technology, including the Internet, to produce, publish, and update individual or shared writing products in response to ongoing feedback, including new arguments or information.*

# Explanation

This standard asks students to use technology for persuasive, informative/explanatory, and narrative texts. No table or graphic organizer is applicable.

## CCSS.ELA-Literacy.W.11-12.7

Conduct short as well as more sustained research projects to answer a question (including a self-generated question) or solve a problem; narrow or broaden the inquiry when appropriate; synthesize multiple sources on the subject, demonstrating understanding of the subject under investigation.*

## Explanation

This standard asks students to find information from various sources for research writing, change the focus if necessary, and summarize research information. With this graphic organizer, students are able to propose a question/problem at the top, identify information from various sources in the top boxes, make sure it is related to their research question at the top, and synthesize information found for the demonstration of understanding in the big box at the bottom. Space is provided to consider narrowing or broadening the inquiry.

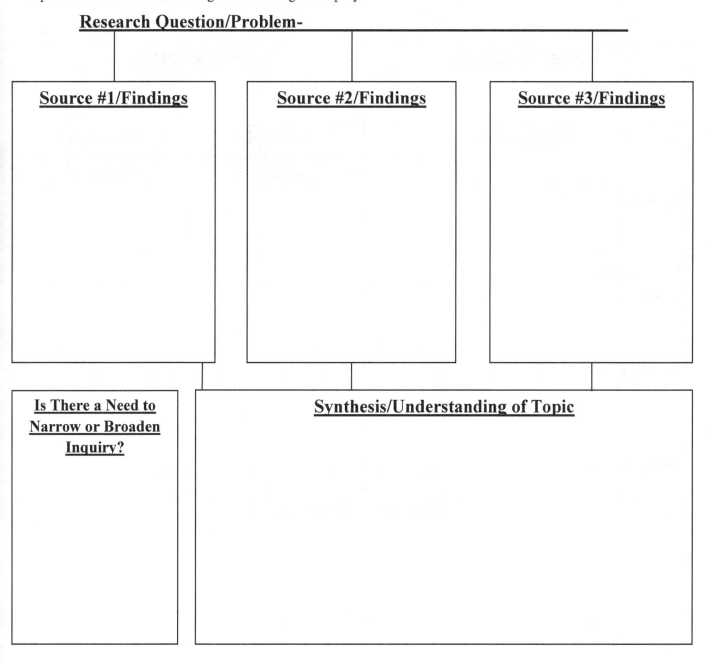

**Research Question/Problem-**

| Source #1/Findings | Source #2/Findings | Source #3/Findings |

**Is There a Need to Narrow or Broaden Inquiry?**

**Synthesis/Understanding of Topic**

# CCSS.ELA-Literacy.W.11-12.8

Gather relevant information from multiple authoritative print and digital sources, using advanced searches effectively; assess the strengths and limitations of each source in terms of the task, purpose, and audience; integrate information into the text selectively to maintain the flow of ideas, avoiding plagiarism and overreliance on any one source and following a standard format for citation.*

# Explanation

This standard asks students to find pertinent information, utilize searches, appraise the value of the information, synthesize the information in a balanced/cohesive manner without plagiarism, and cite sources. With this graphic organizer, students are able to write the research question and brainstorm search terms in the first table, gather information/assess its usefulness and include bibliography in the second table, and integrate information in the third table.

| Research Question: | Search Terms: | |
|---|---|---|

| Information | Strengths (For Task/Purpose/Audience) | Limitations (For Task/Purpose/Audience) |
|---|---|---|
| **Source 1** <br><br><br><br> Bibliography: | | |
| **Source 2** <br><br><br><br> Bibliography: | | |
| **Source 3** <br><br><br><br> Bibliography: | | |

| Integration of Sources 1–3 |
|---|
| |

## CCSS.ELA-Literacy.W.11-12.9

Draw evidence from literary or informational texts to support analysis, reflection, and research.*

## CCSS.ELA-Literacy.W.11-12.9.a

Apply *grades 11–12 Reading standards* to literature (e.g., "Demonstrate knowledge of eighteenth-, nineteenth- and early-twentieth-century foundational works of American literature, including how two or more texts from the same period treat similar themes or topics").*

## CCSS.ELA-Literacy.W.11-12.9.b

Apply *grades 11–12 Reading standards* to literary nonfiction (e.g., "Delineate and evaluate the reasoning in seminal U.S. texts, including the application of constitutional principles and use of legal reasoning [e.g., in U.S. Supreme Court Case majority opinions and dissents] and the premises, purposes, and arguments in works of public advocacy [e.g., *The Federalist*, presidential addresses]").*

## Explanation

This group of standards asks students to write for the purpose of expressing the reading standards. With the first example guide, students are able to link a literature reading standard at the top to related analysis, reflection, and research below it. With the second example guide, students are able to link a literary nonfiction reading standard at the top to related analysis, reflection, and research below it.

## Literature Standard:_____

## Analysis/Reflection/Research:

_____

_____

_____

_____

_____

## Nonfiction Standard:_____

## Analysis/Reflection/Research:

_____

_____

_____

_____

_____

## <u>CCSS.ELA-Literacy.W.11-12.10</u>

Write routinely over extended time frames (time for research, reflection, and revision) and shorter time frames (a single sitting or a day or two) for a range of tasks, purposes, and audiences.*

## <u>Explanation</u>

This standard asks students to write short and long pieces of writing. No table or graphic organizer is applicable.

# CHAPTER 28

# 11th–12th Grade Speaking/Listening

## CCSS.ELA-Literacy.SL.11-12.1

Initiate and participate effectively in a range of collaborative discussions (one-on-one, in groups, and teacher-led) with diverse partners on grades 11–12 topics, texts, and issues, building on others' ideas and expressing their own clearly and persuasively.*

## CCSS.ELA-Literacy.SL.11-12.1.a

Come to discussions prepared, having read and researched material under study; explicitly draw on that preparation by referring to evidence from texts and other research on the topic or issue to stimulate a thoughtful, well-reasoned exchange of ideas.*

## Explanation

This standard asks students to be ready with topical evidence for class discussions. With this graphic organizer, students are able to write the topic/issue at the top and prepare using an outline, a graphic organizer, or both.

**Topic/Issue of Discussion:**

| Evidence From Reading/Studying: | Evidence From Reading/Studying: |
|---|---|
| I.<br>A.<br>B.<br>C.<br><br>II.<br>A.<br>B.<br>C.<br><br>III.<br>A.<br>B.<br>C.<br><br>IV.<br>A.<br>B.<br>C.<br><br>V.<br>A.<br>B.<br>C. | |

## CCSS.ELA-Literacy.SL.11-12.1

Initiate and participate effectively in a range of collaborative discussions (one-on-one, in groups, and teacher-led) with diverse partners on grades 11–12 topics, texts, and issues, building on others' ideas and expressing their own clearly and persuasively.*

## CCSS.ELA-Literacy.SL.11-12.1.b

Work with peers to promote civil, democratic discussions and decision-making, set clear goals and deadlines, and establish individual roles as needed.*

## Explanation

This standard asks students to participate with classmates in setting amicable and self-governing discussion norms. With this graphic organizer, students are able to write the topic/issue at the top, propose rules, goals, deadlines, and roles in the middle column, and work with peers on a consensus for those elements in the right column.

### Topic/Issue of Discussion:

| | Student | Work With Peers |
|---|---|---|
| **Rules** | | |
| **Goals** | | |
| **Deadlines** | | |
| **Individual Roles** | | |

# CCSS.ELA-Literacy.SL.11-12.1

Initiate and participate effectively in a range of collaborative discussions (one-on-one, in groups, and teacher-led) with diverse partners on grades 11–12 topics, texts, and issues, building on others' ideas and expressing their own clearly and persuasively.*

# CCSS.ELA-Literacy.SL.11-12.1.c

Propel conversations by posing and responding to questions that probe reasoning and evidence; ensure a hearing for a full range of positions on a topic or issue; clarify, verify, or challenge ideas and conclusions; and promote divergent and creative perspectives.*

## Explanation

This standard asks students to participate in class discussion with questions and comments that explore reasons/evidence, integrate classmates' views, explain or confront issues, and encourage different and innovative views. With this graphic organizer, students are able to write the topic at the top, pose and respond to questions that probe reasons and evidence in the second row, ensure a hearing for a full range of positions in the third row, clarify/verify/challenge ideas and conclusions in the fourth row, and promote divergent and creative perspectives in the fifth row.

### Topic/Issue of Discussion:

|  | Questions | Responses |
|---|---|---|
| **Probe Reasoning/ Evidence** | | |
| **Ensure a Full Range of Positions/ Perspectives** | | |
| **Clarify/ Verify/ Challenge Ideas and Conclusions** | | |
| **Promote Divergent/ Creative Perspectives** | | |

# CCSS.ELA-Literacy.SL.11-12.1

Initiate and participate effectively in a range of collaborative discussions (one-on-one, in groups, and teacher-led) with diverse partners on grades 11–12 topics, texts, and issues, building on others' ideas and expressing their own clearly and persuasively.*

# CCSS.ELA-Literacy.SL.11-12.1.d

Respond thoughtfully to diverse perspectives; synthesize comments, claims, and evidence made on all sides of an issue; resolve contradictions when possible; and determine what additional information or research is required to deepen the investigation or complete the task.*

# Explanation

This standard asks students to reply to various information communicated in class discussions, integrate that information, fix contradictions, and decide what additional information could help the examination or assignment. With this graphic organizer, students are able to write the topic/issue, their views, and others' views at the top, record responses to diverse perspectives in the first column, synthesize comments/claims/evidence in the second column, resolve contradictions in the third column, and determine what additional information/research is required in the fourth column.

### Topic/Issue of Discussion:

Your View:

_____

_____

Others' Views:

_____

_____

_____

| Responses To Diverse Perspectives | Synthesis of Comments/ Claims/ Evidence | Resolution of Contradictions | Additional Information/ Research Required |
|---|---|---|---|
|  |  |  |  |

## CCSS.ELA-Literacy.SL.11-12.2

Integrate multiple sources of information presented in diverse formats and media (e.g., visually, quantitatively, orally) in order to make informed decisions and solve problems, evaluating the credibility and accuracy of each source and noting any discrepancies among the data.*

## Explanation

This standard asks students to solve problems/make decisions based on various informational material, evaluate each source's reliability and precision, and recognize which sources possess inconsistencies. With this graphic organizer, students are able to write the decision to be made/problem to be solved at the top, identify various information and evaluate credibility/accuracy in the top three boxes, integrate that information in the big box at the bottom, and note discrepancies among the data in the small box at the bottom.

## Decision to be Made/Problem to be Solved:

| Visual | Quantitative | Oral |
|---|---|---|
| a. | a. | a. |
| b. | b. | b. |
| Is it credible/accurate? | Is it credible/accurate? | Is it credible/accurate? |

**Integration of Sources**

**Data Discrepancies**

# CCSS.ELA-Literacy.SL.11-12.3

Evaluate a speaker's point of view, reasoning, and use of evidence and rhetoric, assessing the stance, premises, links among ideas, word choice, points of emphasis, and tone used.*

## Explanation

This standard asks students to assess a speaker's point of view in terms of explanations, proof, word choice, position, assumptions, thought connectivity, language selection, highlighting of ideas, and attitude. With this graphic organizer, students are able to write the speaker's point of view and assess his/her stance taken in the top box, evaluate the reasons, evidence, and rhetoric in the left column, and assess premises, links among ideas, word choice/tone, and points of emphasis in the right column.

| Evaluation of Point of View | Assessment of Stance |
|---|---|
|  |  |

| Evaluation | Assessment |
|---|---|
| Reasons- | Premises- |
| Evidence- | Links Among Ideas- |
| Rhetoric- | Word Choice/Tone- |
|  | Points of Emphasis- |

## CCSS.ELA-Literacy.SL.11-12.4

Present information, findings, and supporting evidence, conveying a clear and distinct perspective, such that listeners can follow the line of reasoning, alternative or opposing perspectives are addressed, and the organization, development, substance, and style are appropriate to purpose, audience, and a range of formal and informal tasks.*

## Explanation

This standard asks students to present a view in terms of connected reasons and evidence. With this graphic organizer, students are able to identify a perspective in the top box, organize/develop the substance of the presentation through reasons/evidence in the middle box, and address alternative/opposing perspectives in the bottom box.

### Perspective

|  |
|  |

↓

### Organization/Development/Substance

| Line of Reasoning | Supporting Evidence |
| --- | --- |
| Reason 1- | Evidence 1- |
| Reason 2- | Evidence 2- |
| Reason 3- | Evidence 3- |

↓

### Alternative/Opposing Perspectives

|  |
|  |

## CCSS.ELA-Literacy.SL.11-12.5

Make strategic use of digital media (e.g., textual, graphical, audio, visual, and interactive elements) in presentations to enhance understanding of findings, reasoning, and evidence and to add interest.*

## Explanation

This standard asks students to incorporate purposeful digital media in class speeches. With this graphic organizer, students are able to brainstorm what they intend to present in the left column, relate what digital media could be utilized in the middle column, and explain how the media enhances understanding/adds interest in the right column.

| Presentation Information (Main Ideas) | Possible Digital Media Components (Textual, Graphical, Audio, Visual, and Interactive) | How the Digital Media Component Enhances Understanding/Adds Interest |
|---|---|---|
| | | |
| | | |
| | | |

## CCSS.ELA-Literacy.SL.11-12.6

Adapt speech to a variety of contexts and tasks, demonstrating a command of formal English when indicated or appropriate. (See grades 11–12 Language standards 1 and 3 here for specific expectations.)*

## Explanation

This standard asks students to speak within a range of grade-level situations. No table or graphic organizer is applicable.

# CHAPTER 29

# 11th–12th Grade
# Language

## CCSS.ELA-Literacy.L.11-12.1

Demonstrate command of the conventions of standard English grammar and usage when writing or speaking.*

## CCSS.ELA-Literacy.L.11-12.1.a

Apply the understanding that usage is a matter of convention, can change over time, and is sometimes contested.*

## Explanation

This standard asks students to utilize the principle that usage is agreed upon, transformed over time, and is disputed. With this graphic organizer, students are able to write a particular usage in the first column, explain how it is a matter of convention in the second column, document how the usage has changed over time in the third column, and relate how it has been contested in the fourth column.

| Usage | Matter of Convention | Change over Time | Contested |
|-------|---------------------|------------------|-----------|
|       |                     |                  |           |
|       |                     |                  |           |

# CCSS.ELA-Literacy.L.11-12.1

Demonstrate command of the conventions of standard English grammar and usage when writing or speaking.*

# CCSS.ELA-Literacy.L.11-12.1.b

Resolve issues of complex or contested usage, consulting references (e.g., *Merriam-Webster's Dictionary of English Usage, Garner's Modern American Usage*) as needed.*

# Explanation

This standard asks students to utilize references, if appropriate, to correctly determine complicated or disputed usage issues. With this graphic organizer, students are able to write the complex or contested usage issue in the left column and relate its resolution, consulting references as needed, in the right column.

| Complex/Complicated Usage Issue | Resolution (from Reference as Needed) |
|---|---|
|  |  |
|  |  |

## CCSS.ELA-Literacy.L.11-12.2

Demonstrate command of the conventions of standard English capitalization, punctuation, and spelling when writing.*

## CCSS.ELA-Literacy.L.11-12.2.a

Observe hyphenation conventions.*

## Explanation

This standard asks students to follow hyphenation conventions. With this example guide, students are given space to discern each of the main hyphenation conventions.

## Hyphen Conventions

**1. To link two or more words that function as a sole adjective before a noun:**

_____

**2. To separate compound numbers:**

_____

**3. To avoid a confusing combination of letters:**

_____

**4. With the prefixes ex-, self-, all-, with the suffix -elect:**

_____

**5. To separate words at the conclusion of a line between syllables:**

_____

_____

## CCSS.ELA-Literacy.L.11-12.2

Demonstrate command of the conventions of standard English capitalization, punctuation, and spelling when writing.*

## CCSS.ELA-Literacy.L.11-12.2.b

Spell correctly.*

## Explanation

This standard asks students to spell words precisely. No table or graphic organizer is applicable.

## CCSS.ELA-Literacy.L.11-12.3

Apply knowledge of language to understand how language functions in different contexts, to make effective choices for meaning or style, and to comprehend more fully when reading or listening.*

## CCSS.ELA-Literacy.L.11-12.3.a

Vary syntax for effect, consulting references (e.g., Tufte's *Artful Sentences*) for guidance as needed; apply an understanding of syntax to the study of complex texts when reading.*

## Explanation

This standard asks students to utilize various arrangements of words for specific results, utilize a reference if needed, and use a comprehension of syntax to understand intricate texts. With this graphic organizer, students are able to use the top table to identify the effect they want to achieve in the left column and relate the syntax they will use to achieve it in the right column, consulting references as needed. Students are able to use the bottom table to demonstrate an understanding of particular syntax in the left column and utilize that understanding in the study of a complex text in the right column.

| Effect | Syntax Used (Use Reference as Needed) |
|---|---|
|  |  |
|  |  |
|  |  |

| Syntax Understanding | Utilization in Complex Text Study |
|---|---|
|  |  |
|  |  |

# CCSS.ELA-Literacy.L.11-12.4

Determine or clarify the meaning of unknown and multiple-meaning words and phrases based on *grades 11–12 reading and content*, choosing flexibly from a range of strategies.*

# CCSS.ELA-Literacy.L.11-12.4.a

Use context (e.g., the overall meaning of a sentence, paragraph, or text; a word's position or function in a sentence) as a clue to the meaning of a word or phrase.*

# Explanation

This standard asks students to utilize context for word definition clues. With this graphic organizer, students are able to write the unknown word or phrase in the left column, relate given clues to its meaning in the middle column, and make an educated guess about its definition in the right column.

| Unknown Word/Phrase | Possible Clue Words/ Overall Meaning/ Position or Function | Possible Meaning of Unknown Word/Phrase |
|---|---|---|
| | | |
| | | |
| | | |
| | | |
| | | |
| | | |
| | | |

## CCSS.ELA-Literacy.L.11-12.4

Determine or clarify the meaning of unknown and multiple-meaning words and phrases based on *grades 11–12 reading and content*, choosing flexibly from a range of strategies.*

## CCSS.ELA-Literacy.L.11-12.4.b

Identify and correctly use patterns of word changes that indicate different meanings or parts of speech (e.g., *conceive, conception, conceivable*).*

## Explanation

This standard asks students to recognize and utilize common word modifications that specify various definitions or parts of speech. With this graphic organizer, students are able to write patterns of words in the left column, each word's different meaning in the middle column, each word's related part of speech in the right column, and use the words correctly in a sentence in the space provided below the table.

| Words | Meaning | Part of Speech |
|-------|---------|----------------|
|       |         |                |
|       |         |                |
|       |         |                |

_____.

_____.

_____.

| Words | Meaning | Part of Speech |
|-------|---------|----------------|
|       |         |                |
|       |         |                |
|       |         |                |

_____.

_____.

_____.

## CCSS.ELA-Literacy.L.11-12.4

Determine or clarify the meaning of unknown and multiple-meaning words and phrases based on *grades 11–12 reading and content*, choosing flexibly from a range of strategies.*

## CCSS.ELA-Literacy.L.11-12.4.c

Consult general and specialized reference materials (e.g., dictionaries, glossaries, thesauruses), both print and digital, to find the pronunciation of a word or determine or clarify its precise meaning, its part of speech, its etymology, or its standard usage.*

## Explanation

This standard asks students to utilize reference resources for unknown words. With this graphic organizer, students are able to write the unknown word in the left column and relate the meaning, part of speech, etymology, standard usage, and/or pronunciation in the right column.

| Unknown Word | Reference Material-Meaning/Part of Speech/Pronunciation/Etymology/Standard Usage |
|---|---|
|  |  |
|  |  |
|  |  |
|  |  |
|  |  |
|  |  |
|  |  |
|  |  |
|  |  |

## CCSS.ELA-Literacy.L.11-12.4

Determine or clarify the meaning of unknown and multiple-meaning words and phrases based on *grades 11–12 reading and content*, choosing flexibly from a range of strategies.*

## CCSS.ELA-Literacy.L.11-12.4.d

Verify the preliminary determination of the meaning of a word or phrase (e.g., by checking the inferred meaning in context or in a dictionary).*

## Explanation

This standard asks students to utilize context and dictionaries for word definition confirmation. With this graphic organizer, students are able to write the unknown word or phrase in the left column, relate its preliminary meaning in the middle column, and verify the definition in the right column.

| Word/Phrase | Preliminary Determination of Meaning | Inferred Meaning in Context/Dictionary |
|---|---|---|
|  |  |  |
|  |  |  |
|  |  |  |
|  |  |  |
|  |  |  |
|  |  |  |
|  |  |  |
|  |  |  |
|  |  |  |
|  |  |  |
|  |  |  |
|  |  |  |
|  |  |  |

# CCSS.ELA-Literacy.L.11-12.5

Demonstrate understanding of figurative language, word relationships, and nuances in word meanings.*

# CCSS.ELA-Literacy.L.11-12.5.a

Interpret figures of speech (e.g., hyperbole, paradox) in context and analyze their role in the text.*

# Explanation

This standard asks students to explain figures of speech and determine their function in a text. With this graphic organizer, students are able to write the figure of speech in the first row, interpret it in the second row, and analyze the figure of speech's role in the text in the third row.

| **Figure of Speech** (Hyperbole, Paradox) | | |
|---|---|---|
| **Interpretation** | | |
| **Role Analysis in Text** | | |

# CCSS.ELA-Literacy.L.11-12.5

Demonstrate understanding of figurative language, word relationships, and nuances in word meanings.*

# CCSS.ELA-Literacy.L.11-12.5.b

Analyze nuances in the meaning of words with similar denotations.*

# Explanation

This standard asks students to determine the subtle definitional differences of related words. With this graphic organizer, students are able to write words with similar denotations in the top row and determine their nuanced meanings in the bottom row.

| Words with Similar Denotations | | | |
|---|---|---|---|
| **Nuanced Meaning** | | | |

| Words with Similar Denotations | | | |
|---|---|---|---|
| **Nuanced Meaning** | | | |

## CCSS.ELA-Literacy.L.11-12.6

Acquire and use accurately general academic and domain-specific words and phrases, sufficient for reading, writing, speaking, and listening at the college and career readiness level; demonstrate independence in gathering vocabulary knowledge when considering a word or phrase important to comprehension or expression.*

## Explanation

This standard asks students to use vocabulary that is grade-level appropriate and collect vocabulary information. For the former, no table or graphic organizer is applicable, and the latter is addressed in CCSS.ELA-Literacy.L.11-12.4.

# CHAPTER 30

# 11th–12th Grade
# History/Social Studies

# CCSS.ELA-Literacy.RH.11-12.1

Cite specific textual evidence to support analysis of primary and secondary sources, connecting insights gained from specific details to an understanding of the text as a whole.*

## Explanation

This standard asks students to indicate proof of examination of primary and secondary sources, with a focus on how wisdom from the text's details helps form a holistic comprehension of the text. With this graphic organizer, students are able to write the primary and secondary sources in the first row, analyze both sources in the second row, relate textual evidence from each source in the third row, determine insights gained from specific details in the fourth row, and use the insights to form an understanding of the whole text in the fifth row.

|  | **Primary Source:** | **Secondary Source:** |
|---|---|---|
| **Analysis** |  |  |
| **Textual Evidence** |  |  |
| **Insights** |  |  |
| **Holistic Understanding** |  |  |

## CCSS.ELA-Literacy.RH.11-12.2

Determine the central ideas or information of a primary or secondary source; provide an accurate summary that makes clear the relationships among the key details and ideas.*

## Explanation

This standard asks students to decide the essential ideas of a primary or secondary source and how important ideas and details relate, then summarize. With this graphic organizer, students are able to write the source name at the top, express the central ideas in the big boxes, and relate how key ideas and details relate in the small boxes below. Space is provided for a summary as well.

## Source:

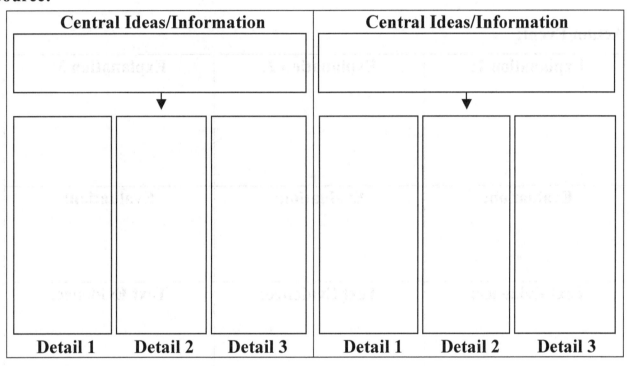

| Central Ideas/Information | | | Central Ideas/Information | | |
| --- | --- | --- | --- | --- | --- |
| Detail 1 | Detail 2 | Detail 3 | Detail 1 | Detail 2 | Detail 3 |

## Summary:

_____

_____

_____

_____

_____

## <u>CCSS.ELA-Literacy.RH.11-12.3</u>

Evaluate various explanations for actions or events and determine which explanation best accords with textual evidence, acknowledging where the text leaves matters uncertain.*

## <u>Explanation</u>

This standard asks students to assess various descriptions of actions and events by deciding which explanation is most supported with textual evidence and recognizing which issues are still vague. With this graphic organizer, students are able to write the action/event at the top, identify explanations for the action or event in the first row, evaluate them in the second row, relate textual evidence in the third row, acknowledge uncertainties in the fourth row, and determine which explanation best accords with textual evidence in the bottom box.

### Action/Event:

| Explanation 1: | Explanation 2: | Explanation 3: |
|---|---|---|
| Evaluation: | Evaluation: | Evaluation: |
| Text Evidence: | Text Evidence: | Text Evidence: |
| Uncertainties: | Uncertainties: | Uncertainties: |

**Which Explanation Best Accords with Textual Evidence? Why?**

## <u>CCSS.ELA-Literacy.RH.11-12.4</u>

Determine the meaning of words and phrases as they are used in a text, including analyzing how an author uses and refines the meaning of a key term over the course of a text (e.g., how Madison defines *faction* in *Federalist* No. 10).*

## <u>Explanation</u>

This standard asks students to establish meanings for words and phrases in a historical/social text and examine how the author utilizes and clarifies its connotation throughout a text. With this graphic organizer, students are able to write the word or phrase in the left column, establish the word's or phrase's meaning in the middle column, and analyze how an author uses and refines the meaning of the key term over the course of a text in the right column.

| Word/ Phrase | Meaning | Analysis of How an Author Uses and Refines the Meaning of the Key Term Over the Course of the Text |
|---|---|---|
| | | |
| | | |

# CCSS.ELA-Literacy.RH.11-12.5

Analyze in detail how a complex primary source is structured, including how key sentences, paragraphs, and larger portions of the text contribute to the whole.*

## Explanation

This standard asks students to examine how a primary source's structure utilizes its parts that contribute to the whole. With this graphic organizer, students are able to write the primary source at the top, identify the text structure in the left column, highlight key sentences, paragraphs, and larger portions of the text in the middle column, and determine how those text section(s) contribute to the whole in the right column.

**Primary Source:**

| Structural Analysis of Primary Source Text (Choose One: Chronological/Sequence, Cause/Effect, Problem/Solution, Compare/Contrast, Description, Directions) | Key Sentences/ Paragraphs/Sections | Contribution to the Whole |
|---|---|---|
|  |  |  |

## CCSS.ELA-Literacy.RH.11-12.6

Evaluate authors' differing points of view on the same historical event or issue by assessing the authors' claims, reasoning, and evidence.*

## Explanation

This standard asks students to assess historical/social authors' divergent points of view in terms of claims, reasons, and evidence. With this graphic organizer, students are able to write the event/issue at the top, identify the authors' points of view in the top boxes, relate their claims, reasons, and evidence in the left columns, and evaluate them in the right columns.

**Event/Issue:**

### Author 1 Point of View

| Author's Elements | Evaluation |
|---|---|
| Claims- | |
| Reasons- | |
| Evidence- | |

### Author 2 Point of View

| Author's Elements | Evaluation |
|---|---|
| Claim- | |
| Reasons- | |
| Evidence- | |

## CCSS.ELA-Literacy.RH.11-12.7

Integrate and evaluate multiple sources of information presented in diverse formats and media (e.g., visually, quantitatively, as well as in words) in order to address a question or solve a problem.*

## Explanation

This standard asks students to combine and assess various historical/social material as a response to an inquiry or an answer to a dilemma. With this graphic organizer, students are able to write the question/problem at the top, identify multiple sources of information in the top three boxes, evaluate each source in the middle three boxes, and integrate all information in the bottom box.

### Question/Problem to Be Solved:

| Visual | Quantitative | Verbal |
|---|---|---|
| a.<br><br>b.<br><br>c.<br><br>d. | a.<br><br>b.<br><br>c.<br><br>d. | a.<br><br>b.<br><br>c.<br><br>d. |
| **Evaluation** | **Evaluation** | **Evaluation** |

| Integration |
|---|
|  |

## CCSS.ELA-Literacy.RH.11-12.8

Evaluate an author's premises, claims, and evidence by corroborating or challenging them with other information.*

## Explanation

This standard asks students to assess a historical/social author's assumptions, arguments, and proof by either confirming or disputing it with other data. With this graphic organizer, students are able to identify an author's premises, claims, and evidence in the left column and either corroborate or challenge them with other information in the right column.

| Author's Elements | Corroboration/Challenge |
|---|---|
| Premise- | Other Information- |
| Claims- | |
| Evidence- | |

# CCSS.ELA-Literacy.RH.11-12.9

Integrate information from diverse sources, both primary and secondary, into a coherent understanding of an idea or event, noting discrepancies among sources.*

## Explanation

This standard asks students to combine information and highlight inconsistencies between primary and secondary sources into a full comprehension of an idea or event. With this graphic organizer, students are able to write the idea/event at the top, identify information from primary and secondary sources in the top two boxes, note discrepancies for each source in the middle two boxes, and integrate all information into a coherent understanding of the idea/event in the bottom box.

**Idea/Event:**

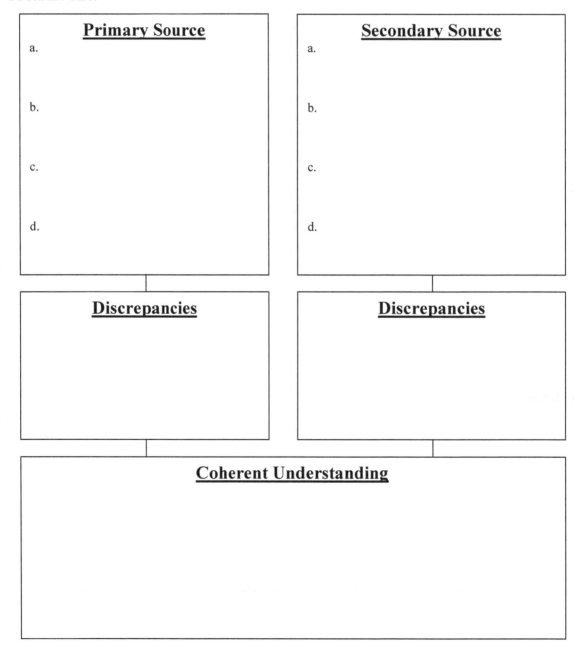

## CCSS.ELA-Literacy.RH.11-12.10

By the end of grade 12, read and comprehend history/social studies texts in the grades 11–CCR text complexity band independently and proficiently.*

## Explanation

This standard asks students to read historical/social texts that are grade-level appropriate. No table or graphic organizer is applicable.

CHAPTER 31

# 11th–12th Grade
# Science/Technical

## CCSS.ELA-Literacy.RST.11-12.1

Cite specific textual evidence to support analysis of science and technical texts, attending to important distinctions the author makes and to any gaps or inconsistencies in the account.*

## Explanation

This standard asks students to indicate proof of examination of scientific/technical texts with a focus on key discrepancies and deviations. With this graphic organizer, students are able to analyze in the first row, relate textual evidence in the second row, identify important distinctions in the third row, and identify inconsistencies/gaps in the fourth row.

| | |
|---|---|
| **Analysis** | |
| **Textual Evidence** | |
| **Important Distinctions** | |
| **Inconsistencies/Gaps** | |

## CCSS.ELA-Literacy.RST.11-12.2

Determine the central ideas or conclusions of a text; summarize complex concepts, processes, or information presented in a text by paraphrasing them in simpler but still accurate terms.*

## Explanation

This standard asks students to establish the essential understandings of a scientific/technical text, then summarize them in their own words. With this graphic organizer, students are able to write the central ideas/conclusions in the top box, document complex concepts, processes, or information in the left column, and paraphrase them in the right column.

### Central Ideas/Conclusions

| Complex Concepts, Processes, or Information | Paraphrased Summary |
|---|---|
|  |  |

## CCSS.ELA-Literacy.RST.11-12.3

Follow precisely a complex multistep procedure when carrying out experiments, taking measurements, or performing technical tasks; analyze the specific results based on explanations in the text.*

## Explanation

This standard asks students to adhere to a scientific/technical process with a focus on examining the outcomes specific to a text's description. With this graphic organizer, students are able to write the name of the procedure at the top, document the procedure in a multistep format in the boxes, and analyze the explanations and results in the table at the bottom.

### Procedure:

1)

2)

3)

4)

5)

6)

| Text's Explanations | Result Analysis |
|---|---|
|  |  |

## CCSS.ELA-Literacy.RST.11-12.4

Determine the meaning of symbols, key terms, and other domain-specific words and phrases as they are used in a specific scientific or technical context relevant to *grades 11–12 texts and topics.**

## Explanation

This standard asks students to establish meanings for symbols, words, and phrases in a scientific/technical text. With this graphic organizer, students are able to write the symbol, word, or phrase in the left column and relate its meaning in the right column.

| Word/ Phrase/Symbol | Meaning |
|---|---|
|  |  |
|  |  |
|  |  |
|  |  |

*The Visual Edge*<sup>©</sup>

# CCSS.ELA-Literacy.RST.11-12.5

Analyze how the text structures information or ideas into categories or hierarchies, demonstrating understanding of the information or ideas.*

# Explanation

This standard asks students to examine how a scientific/technical text's organization of concepts or data is broken down based on grouping or ranking. With this graphic organizer, students are able to identify a text's information and ideas in the left column and analyze its structure (categorical or hierarchical) in the right column.

| Information/Ideas | Structural Analysis |
|---|---|
| | **Categorical**<br><br>Category 1-<br><br>Category 2-<br><br>Category 3-<br><br>Category 4- |
| | **Hierarchical**<br><br> |

## CCSS.ELA-Literacy.RST.11-12.6

Analyze the author's purpose in providing an explanation, describing a procedure, or discussing an experiment in a text, identifying important issues that remain unresolved.*

## Explanation

This standard asks students to examine an author's purpose in a scientific/technical text and recognize significant points that remain unanswered. With this graphic organizer, students are able to identify the author's purpose in the left column, analyze it in the right column, and identify important issues that remain unresolved at the bottom.

| Author's Purpose (Choose One: Providing an Explanation, Describing a Procedure, or Discussing an Experiment) | Purpose Analysis |
|---|---|
|  |  |
|  |  |

## Important Issues that Remain Unresolved:

-

-

-

## CCSS.ELA-Literacy.RST.11-12.7

Integrate and evaluate multiple sources of information presented in diverse formats and media (e.g., quantitative data, video, multimedia) in order to address a question or solve a problem.*

## Explanation

This standard asks students to combine and assess various scientific/technical materials as a response to an inquiry or an answer to a dilemma. With this graphic organizer, students are able to write the question/problem at the top, find multiple sources of information in the top three boxes, evaluate each source in the middle three boxes, and integrate all information in the bottom box.

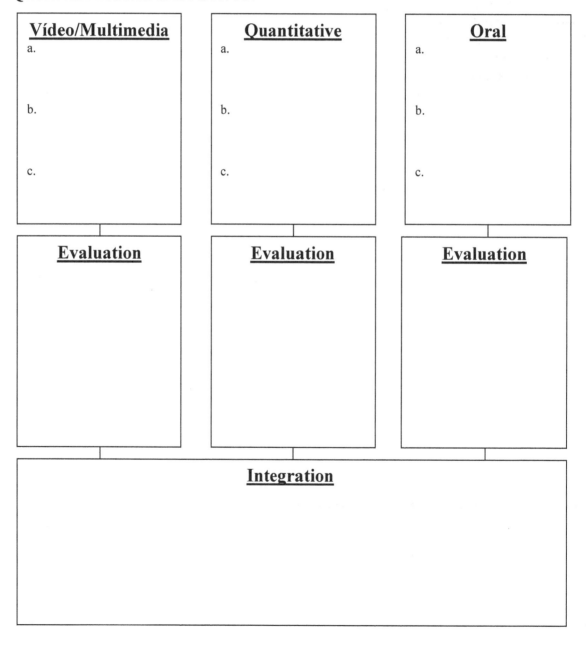

**Question/Problem to Be Solved:**

| Video/Multimedia | Quantitative | Oral |
|---|---|---|
| a. | a. | a. |
| b. | b. | b. |
| c. | c. | c. |

| Evaluation | Evaluation | Evaluation |
|---|---|---|

**Integration**

# CCSS.ELA-Literacy.RST.11-12.8

Evaluate the hypotheses, data, analysis, and conclusions in a science or technical text, verifying the data when possible and corroborating or challenging conclusions with other sources of information.*

## Explanation

This standard asks students to assess educated guesses, information, examination, and judgments in a scientific/technical text by authenticating the information and confirming or disputing outcomes with other data. With this graphic organizer, students are able to use the top table to identify hypotheses and analysis in the left column and evaluate them in the right column. Students are able to use the middle table to identify data in the left column, evaluate it in the middle column, and verify the data in the right column. Students are able to use the bottom table to identify conclusions in the left column, evaluate them in the middle column, and corroborate or challenge the conclusions in the right column.

| Information | Evaluation |
|---|---|
| **Hypotheses** | |
| **Analysis** | |

| Information | Evaluation | Verification |
|---|---|---|
| **Data** | | (Other Source Information: _____ _____) |

| Information | Evaluation | Corroborate or Challenge |
|---|---|---|
| **Conclusions** | | (Other Source Information: _____ _____) |

## CCSS.ELA-Literacy.RST.11-12.9

Synthesize information from a range of sources (e.g., texts, experiments, simulations) into a coherent understanding of a process, phenomenon, or concept, resolving conflicting information when possible.*

## Explanation

This standard asks students to combine various scientific/technical material into a logical comprehension of a procedure, trend, or principle and determine any inconsistencies that may exist. With this graphic organizer, students are able to choose the information type at the top, identify information from various sources in the top three boxes, resolve conflicting information in the middle box, and synthesize all information in the bottom box.

### Information Type (Choose: Process, Phenomenon, or Concept)

| **Texts** | **Experiments** | **Simulations** |
|---|---|---|
| a. | a. | a. |
| b. | b. | b. |
| c. | c. | c. |

### Resolution of Conflicting Information

### Synthesis to Demonstrate Coherent Understanding

# CCSS.ELA-Literacy.RST.11-12.10

By the end of grade 12, read and comprehend science/technical texts in the grades 11–CCR text complexity band independently and proficiently.*

# Explanation

This standard asks students to read scientific/technical texts that are grade-level appropriate. No table or graphic organizer is applicable.

# NOTES

1.  Bradford, William C., "Reaching the Visual Learner: Teaching Property Through Art (September 1, 2011)." *The Law Teacher* Vol. 11, 2004.

2.  The Institute for the Advancement of Research in Education (IARE) at AEL: "Graphic Organizers: A Review of Scientifically Based Research," July 2003.

CPSIA information can be obtained
at www.ICGtesting.com
Printed in the USA
LVHW10s1156241018
594614LV00011B/102/P